OUR HOME, OUR PASSION

A Build-It-Yourself Memoir

Elaine C. McGee

Acknowledgments

To my kids, Paul, Suzanne, Diane and Phillip, all of whom have had a hand in encouraging, as well as criticizing, my Build-It-Yourself Memoir. I'm grateful to James Keller, Elizabeth Balderson and Lois Larson for their editing efforts and to the many friends who have commented on my rough draft. I am especially indebted to Phillip, who has shown great patience in helping to edit and design the manuscript and integrate our plans and pictures; to his wife Lynne, for the cover design, and to Diane for a final polish. Readers will note that very few pictures of the original house survived; hopefully the narrative will suffice to illustrate its many charms.

I would like to dedicate this book to all those who have lost their homes in the recent wildfires.

TABLE OF CONTENTS - PART I: 1948-1991

TABLE OF CONTENTS - PART II: 1991 TO NOW

By Way of Introduction

In 1950, I refused the home editor of the Oakland Tribune permission to write the story of how we built a $100,000 home for $10,000 in the Oakland-Berkeley hills of California. I felt that was my tale to tell to veterans who needed affordable housing after World War II. It has taken me six decades to tell the story, but now my goal has changed. After losing our home in the firestorm of 1991, I want to encourage other Californians who have lost their homes to wildfires to rebuild again.

I also want to honor my husband Henry, without whose fearless spirit, awesome intelligence and extraordinary expertise our home would not have gotten off the ground. And I want to pay homage to our architect, Robert Weaver Stevens, a creative genius, who cared as much about design as Frank Lloyd Wright, but even more about kitchens and bathrooms.

Henry gained his understanding of the building process by reading "how to" books and the <u>Popular Mechanics</u> magazine. He also had the experience, while in junior college, of breaking up concrete for the street department of Pasadena. My husband modestly credits his manual training course in junior high and the two-foot wall he built around his mother's garden in Pasadena for his know-how. But I'm convinced it was his remarkable kinesthetic sense that made it possible for him to perform, with ease and grace, whatever building skill was required.

1

The dubious talent I brought to our partnership was the ability to scrounge for materials, a skill I picked up in the Navy, where I collected a library for the Advanced Base Training School. I found it an easy switch from gathering books from the East/West Association and submarine pamphlets from a secret naval facility below the streets of New York, to collecting 40-foot wooden beams and secondhand plate glass in Berkeley, California.

After the arduous year it took to build our home, we thought nothing could lure us from our perch on the hill. When Henry received his doctorate in 1952, we were put to the test. Would we, as the saying goes, live to work or work to live? There was no contest. To remain in our just-built home, Henry turned down the rare opportunity to help found Evergreen University in the state of Washington. Years later, after a number of sabbaticals abroad, with the horrendous problems we encountered in renting our home, Henry wondered if we should sell. The answer was "no." When we built a smaller house across the road to protect our view and were offered a fortune for our original house, the answer was still "no".

Needless to say, we found pioneering on our one and a half acres a challenging and sometimes hazardous adventure, but thrilling and financially rewarding. Perhaps we were rare birds in the twentieth century. We not only had the deep-seated desire, but also the luxury, of living in our home for a lifetime. This is a tale of building for a way of life, losing it all and gaining it once again.

This is the Place

We rolled out of bed the morning after our wedding. It was Saturday, February 14, 1948, and we were raring to find a building site in the undeveloped hills of Berkeley, California. After four years in the Navy during World War II, Henry was thirty-five and I was twenty-eight, and time was a-wasting. We wanted a home and kids and right away.

Location, in our lexicon, meant view, space and country, within the city limits. And there it was, 1400 feet above sea level, with a panorama of the Bay, the bridges and San Francisco. The property bordered the East Bay Regional parklands, where the coastal fog rims the hilltops, protecting and creating eternal spring below. Remote and unspoiled as this area was, we clocked eight minutes driving time to the University of California. We had come home. Surely, with fifty acres, the owner would be willing to part with a small piece of her property. Confronting a formidable gate and a fierce police dog, we weren't daunted, especially since the barefooted woman standing behind the gate seemed so outgoing and friendly. But there we

3

stood, locked out physically and emotionally as she explained, "My husband and I were going to build a great home on this mountaintop when I learned that his airplane had crashed in Palm Springs. I have no intention of parting with even a tiny portion of our mountain, ever."

Afterwards, instead of understanding her loss and grief, I said to Henry, "Darling, how can she sit on all that land and feel comfortable when we have none at all?"

Henry was more realistic. "Property owners are all of a kind - possessive, protective and exclusive. You'll be, too."

Today I realize how perceptive he was. We are sitting on one and a half acres and I wouldn't give one inch of it away, except to our kids when we die. But at least we knew this undeveloped area fulfilled our dreams, and we would explore it until we found our niche.

After that first rebuff, we stopped feeling orphaned and sorry for ourselves. We became adept at tracking down property owners at the county courthouse, as well as recognizing monuments in the road and assessing easements and boundaries. One day we hiked over to the next hill and stumbled upon a site, which for us, dwarfed Mrs. Varney's mountaintop.

This property led us to Stanley Hiller, a creative entrepreneur who told us if we wanted a special piece of his property, we would have to buy the entire fifty acres for fifty thousand dollars. He added, to ease our apparent distress, "I'll even throw in ten

4

acres in the bottom of the canyon for a clubhouse and tennis courts."

Fifty thousand dollars for land, even for fifty acres, sounded like fifty million to us. Besides, the dirt roads were crumbling and there were no utilities. But we wanted that site. We talked to the engineer who'd planned the original development. He warned us that the dirt roads would have to be stabilized before paving. So intent were we on acquiring the property, even that didn't deter us.

Henry made a topographical model of the entire area out of plywood, which was very effective, but extremely heavy. Nevertheless, we lugged it around, letting our friends choose their two and a half acre lots, only retaining our special site for ourselves. Every one of our friends were enthusiastic about the project and wanted in, except my father in the East, who suggested we were sashaying upon ground that even well-heeled experienced developers might hesitate to tread. We knew we were in deep, but persisted relentlessly.

One day we drove by what only could be described as a sylvan meadow in a protected area of the Uplands, eight hundred feet below the site we wanted, with no bay view and bordering the old Sacramento railroad. However, it did have surfaced roads and utilities. By this time we had ten couples interested in the Hiller property, but that was far from our goal of twenty-four. We rang the bell of a little house next to the acreage.

The oldest living resident in the area, or so he seemed to us, spoke bluntly, "You youngsters

couldn't afford what I'm asking for my four acres."
Almost as an aside he added, "Why don't you go up
the hill on Grand View Drive? There you will find a
property where I used to go berrying as a kid. It has
a benign climate, a glorious bay view, oak trees, a
canyon, and, of course, blackberries." He even drew
us a map. We set off at once, eager to view the
land he said was paradise.

We stood at the top of Grand View Drive and
Live Oak Road, looking down through the tangle of
greasewood, poison oak and towering oaks, and
knew as surely as Brigham Young knew when he
saw his site in Utah, "This is the Place."

"This is the place"

We tore off the 'For Sale' sign that was nailed to
a tree and went down the hill to call the posted
number. The little German woman who owned the
lot wanted eighteen hundred dollars and we agreed

6

that was a fair price, although we would have paid anything she asked. After taking pictures of our property, we drove across country in our Crosley to show my family our home site with its panoramic view.

When we returned from the East and received our title search report, we realized we had bought a piece of the back canyon. The view side was owned by someone else, and just who that could be was enshrouded in mystery. Whoever it was paid his tax bill in person, so there was no forwarding address recorded at the tax office.

We became dogged detectives. The difficulty in locating the owner had to do with a number of conflicting facts, since he had retired and had no living relatives. Along with those obstacles, there had been a change of name and address. We did learn that he was on a trip to Europe, but turned up little else.

Nevertheless, we persisted in our search, which took us to swank San Francisco neighborhoods and doormen who gave us clues, most of them worthless. Finally, in the third month of our search, a lead found us ringing the doorbell of a lovely home in St. Francis Wood.

An elderly gentleman opened the door, and in answer to our question about the lot in the Berkeley Hills, called to his wife, "Sweetheart, there are two kiddies here who want to buy your goat hill."

We finally learned the reason for our difficulty in tracking down the Giddings. All his life, Horace J. Giddings had had a hard time accepting the name

Horace. When he retired as an executive of the United Fruit Company, he decided to become Jack H. Giddings. Even though Horace's conflicted relationship with his name had caused us much anxiety and delay, I couldn't find it in my heart to blame him.

Mrs. Giddings seemed interested. "Why don't you think about the property and I'll talk to my financial advisor. I'm only interested in getting back my original investment."

She mentioned that roads had been built and lots sold in the early l920s as a way for San Franciscans to escape the city in the summer to this fairyland in the upper Claremont area in the Berkeley-Oakland hills. And then the Depression came, leaving the land fallow.

We left elated. We reasoned vacant land up in the hills decades ago couldn't have been worth much. Meanwhile, we were skeptical enough to go to the water company to be sure 'our' property had water. The official scanned the large map that hung on the wall behind him, then turned to us and shook his head sadly. "You wouldn't want to build up there on Grand View Drive where there's no water."

I was crushed by his pronouncement, but Henry was not to be put off. All our tramping the hills, consulting county maps and inquiring about easements, boundaries and monuments in the roads had given him a sophistication and savvy about property that few laymen had. "Please double check. There's a shut off valve in the street bordering the property, so there must be water up there."

Showing his impatience, the official told us to wait and disappeared. When we had just about decided he had dismissed us, he returned red-faced. "I'm sorry I took so long, but I had to go back in our files to a 1922 map. EBMUD had put water lines in, but with no development up there, the pipes had rusted out and were taken off the current maps. So you're in luck. Since we had taken over the water lines, we'll have to put in new lines with no cost to you."

We wasted no time in making a date with the Giddings. However, when we arrived, Jack didn't want to have anything to do with the deal and excused himself. Fortunately, Mrs. Giddings had a shoebox on her lap and was ready to get down to business. As she flipped through her papers, she exclaimed, "I can't understand why I made such a frightful investment. Taxes and interest over the years, as well as the original cost of the lot have mounted up to quite a sum." Before we could register our dismay, she continued, "I'm so annoyed with myself for holding on to this property all these years, I intend to sell it to you for whatever you can afford to pay."

Since we had already bought the canyon lot, we said one thousand dollars would make it possible for us to start building. She seemed very pleased with the transaction and, with charitable grace, wished us luck. Leaving their Rolls and chauffeur at home, we all piled into our little Crosley and putted over the Bay Bridge to the title company in Oakland. When we returned the Giddings to St. Francis Wood, we celebrated the sale with a glass of sherry.

It wasn't until much later, looking back at Mr. Giddings' embarrassment and Mrs. Giddings' willingness to settle for so little, that we figured they may have been told there was no water in those hills, but we rather like to think that they wanted to help a young couple get started. In any case, we were forever grateful to them and ecstatic at our good fortune.

Getting Started

Now that we had acquired our panoramic site, we were eager to devote whatever it took to achieve the home and lifestyle we wanted. But first we had to clear the property of the underbrush to see the lay of the land. We barged right in, piling coyote brush and all kinds of weeds on the perimeter of the lot. We were naive enough to think that burning was an efficient way to rid ourselves of the mountain of brush we had accumulated. I am stunned when I think how cavalier we were in those days, as we resorted to pouring gasoline on the brush to get it started, without even a fire engine standing by. Instead, we stood close to the raging fire as the flames from the prevailing western winds wafted the smoke toward us.

We were fortunate that the wind was gentle that day so we didn't set the mountain on fire. The only victims were us. For weeks we were covered with sores, both internally and externally. That's how we learned that burning poison oak makes it especially virulent. Henry went to school without putting socks over his oozing ankles and I showered in steaming hot water every two hours, which gave me ecstatic relief from the itching but spread the poison oak and destroyed my skin all at the same time. We assured each other that our agony was worthwhile as we saved a ten-foot sapling amidst all the coyote brush we cut. That little oak surely would have been sacrificed under the bulldozer's blade.

designing houses, using sugar cubes for bricks, which he rented to banks for their windows. In college he created the Cal hat that perched on the head of Pacifica at the World's Fair. On his aircraft carrier in World War II, he decorated the Captain's cabin. And now he was designing movie sets and homes in Hollywood. Without a moment's hesitation we asked him to come up to see our property and design our home.

We wanted an aesthetically pleasing home. We wanted to enjoy all views: the bay, the oaks, the canyon, the mountain. We wanted access to the out of doors from every room. We wanted a home that would take little upkeep. I especially wanted a great fireplace as I had grown up with fake ones. Bob's conception exceeded all our requirements by far.

When I first saw the painting Bob made of our home nestled among the oaks and studied his plans, which were deceptively simple, all I could think of was Michelangelo's Adam touching the hand of God in the Sistine Chapel. It was that impressive. So thrilled were we, at the least provocation, we would spread the plans on the pavement for our friends to see.

To our dismay, we quickly learned that our magnificent contemporary house design would not pass muster for a Federal Housing Loan, unless we made lackluster changes to conform to their regulations. That we would not do, and that's when we determined to build our home for the ten thousand dollars we had saved between us.

14

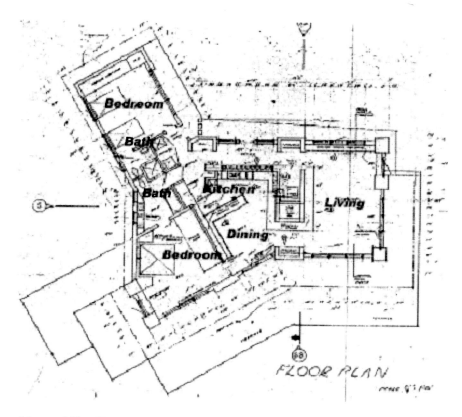

FLOOR PLAN

How We Became Owner-Builders

With our precious plans in tow, we proudly and confidently strode into the City Planning Commission, only to be told by an officious bureaucrat that Bob Stevens' magnificently drawn projections, along with his ten onion skins covering the essential details for making our dream home a reality, were insufficient to acquire a building permit. We were lectured to about the need for many more engineering details and a full set of specifications.

Meanwhile, Bob had gone back to Hollywood, having insisted that his design was his belated wedding present to us. This helps to explain why

15

such an exceptionally talented and generous genius, who created beauty wherever he went, would eventually die a pauper. In any case, we felt it unfair to ask him for more drawings. Instead, we turned to Fran Bryan, our engineer, to do all the necessary structural details that were missing in Bob's drawings. That's what gave us not only Bob's architectural gem but also one of the most stable structures in the hills.

To this day, we strongly recommend to anyone who wants our advice that they get a talented artist/architect to design the concept and an engineer to do the structural details. We have become more convinced than ever of the soundness of this approach as we view the rebuilt monstrosities on our hill, where attention to design is the last consideration and sheer bulk and size seem to be the highest priority.

We were up to the wee hours trying to write specs for our home. Realizing how ill equipped we were to handle this exercise, we frequented Bay Area libraries and book stores, talked to builders and collected information on all kinds of building materials from construction companies. What made this project all the more challenging was our desire to specify top quality materials, knowing that we intended to put the plans out to bid for the modest sum of ten thousand dollars.

We thought our problem was solved when Tommy Boothe, our radiant heat man, recommended a general contractor who lived in our neighborhood. He assured us that Maxwell would allow us to work with him so we could build a good house for our limited bucks. And so we signed an agreement for time and materials, with the understanding that our limit was ten thousand dollars and, with our labor, we would be able to lower costs wherever possible.

I remember our first meeting with the contractor and feeling in awe of how knowledgeable Henry, Bob and Tommy were as they discussed the plans for this unusual contemporary home, even though it was all Greek to me. I did speak with authority when I saw that the radiant heat scheme placed pipes under the floor of our closet. That, I didn't want. Why, I don't know; our huge walk-in closet would prove unendurably cold during the winter months.

During the first two weeks I went up to the lot frequently to check on the progress. Except for a few wooden stakes scattered about, nothing seemed to be happening. Finally, in the third week, I learned from our contractor that the ground was so hard he couldn't lay out the house with the usual wooden stakes. As a result, he had been running all over San Francisco to locate and rent iron stakes. For this we had been paying him contractor's wages for three weeks. I ventured that I was a good scavenger and beseeched him to call on me for such errands.

Within the next week, a whole batch of No. 1 lumber was delivered to the site. Delirious with excitement, I called Henry at school, interrupting his principal's meeting to announce that, at long last, we were on our way. The next afternoon I came up to see three carpenters carefully measuring our No. 1 lumber - for an outhouse.

At the end of the week, I found ten laborers digging trenches for the foundation. Again, my spirits soared - until Monday, when I arrived to see the same chaps leaning on their shovels, not knowing where to go from there.

That's when I made a call on Mr. Maxwell at his home. He greeted me in smoking jacket with mint julep in hand. Needless to say, I was speechless with rage and he seemed slightly embarrassed, as he assured me he would be up to supervise his men, *pronto*.

Henry and I were too green to know that the best course of action when dealing with a 'lemon' was to pay him off immediately. Instead, we struggled on and on as labor and material costs rose. The foundation phase seemed never ending, gobbling up much more of our dollars than we had reckoned for that operation.

When Henry could stand the procrastination no longer, he gave Maxwell an ultimatum. "The foundation must be poured this coming Monday." Maxwell stuttered and pointed to a pile of dirt that had to be leveled first. "Order the cement. The ground will be leveled and ready," roared Henry. That weekend my husband did the work of ten of Maxwell's laborers and it was ready to go.

A rugged cement crew arrived on the job early Monday morning. When they finished pouring, we gave them a send-off with a case of beer and informed Maxwell we had decided to build ourselves. We watched as the crew piled our shovels and brooms, along with theirs, onto their trucks and drove off. Even that didn't bother us. We were free, free at last.

The next day we drove to San Leandro to get a new product we had read about for waterproofing foundations. In an old shack behind the fellow's house we bought gallons of the stuff. When we mentioned we were owner builders, the proprietor discounted the price by fifty percent.

From that moment on, there was no question in our minds that we really were in charge, and that we would and could and should build our own home.

To be so cavalier about taking on the building of our home because we encountered an incompetent contractor could have turned into a risky enterprise. However, we were fortunate that Henry, a school principal, and I, a grad student on the GI bill, had after-school hours, vacations and our summer free to devote to our building project.

Still, there were moments when as amateur builders our reach exceeded our grasp. One of those times occurred on a bitter, blustery night. That evening, like most after-school hours, I mixed cement and Henry climbed up the ladder with a bucket to pour the cores of our block wall. Especially tired that night, I couldn't wait to finish washing the tools in the wheel barrel when I glanced over at Henry, who was frantically trying to scoop out from the cores the cement he had just poured. Ambling over to steady the ladder, which was wobbling from his vigorous scraping, I shouted, "What are you doing up there? Come on down. I'm cold and it's too dark to do anything more tonight."

"Damn it, sweetheart, I've got to clean out these cores before the cement sets up!" Realizing that the cement had already set, he descended the ladder, sighed deeply, put his arms around me and moaned, "I've just poured the flue."

"What does that mean?"

"Only that I've ruined our house."

We stood there clinging to each other as though our world had come to an end. Neither of us said a word as we left our 'ruins' and went back to the little eagle's nest we were renting. We ate some cornflakes and fell into bed to roil inward until daylight.

In the middle of the night, Henry jumped out of bed and started looking through photographs we had taken of our building progress. There it was, a picture clearly showing a flue sticking up above the then four-foot wall. Before dawn, we were on our way back to our site.

With flashlight and photograph in hand, we located the exact core. Henry bored into the wall and found, to our profound relief, that he had stuffed the pipe with newspaper, thus saving our plumbing system and our home.

The Little Engine That Could

To this day, I am awed that we pioneered on our pristine hill to build our own house. It never would have happened if I hadn't married the original do-it-yourself chap. I found this out on our honeymoon trip across the country in a Crosley.

That trip set the stage for our hilarious do-it-yourself adventures for the next half century. We lost four clutches en route. After the second clutch went out, I was ready to ditch the car, hitch or bike. Not Henry. When the last clutch gave up in Pennsylvania, he had the mechanics down to a system. While he dove under the car to unhitch the clutch, I thumbed into the nearest town, and was back with the clutch plate just as he was ready to button up the engine. It took us exactly four hours. We floated the last leg of our trip to Southern Jersey, even overtaking a Stanley Steamer, the only car we passed on the whole trip.

The log of our trip, recorded on the back of our U.S map, pinpointed our trials. Ten cents, ice cream cones; ten dollars, clutch plate; twenty-five cents, watermelon; seventy-five dollars, clutch. We had intended to camp, see the country, attend a teacher's conference in Detroit and end up in my family's place in Atlantic City, New Jersey.

We never made the conference and all we ever saw of our great country was the underside of the Crosley. We could have gone to Paris for what it cost us to patch up our car.

which had won the blue ribbon at the festival. This was Henry's wedding gift to me. Those moccasins cost more than the return trip and I swore I'd wear them the rest of my life, until… but I'm getting ahead of my story. First, a significant character in our little drama wants to have his say.

The Crosley's Tale

My life with the McGee family began in 1948 when Elaine picked me out at the car agency in San Jose. I was extremely proud to be selected from all the others, until I heard her say to Henry, "I guess I'll have to settle for that little sewing machine, as there really isn't any other choice I can afford and I must have transportation for my teaching job in Lafayette."

Any other choice indeed! She should have been grateful to Mr. Crosley who, so soon after the war, was able to transform his light airplane engine into an automobile that could run on so little gas and be sold so cheaply.

I know Elaine cared a lot about me and went into great detail to record our horrendous trip across country and back, a trip I have no interest in remembering. But, no matter, my productive life began in earnest when we started building. Without me, they never would have made it.

She would load me up with heavy cement blocks that had to be cut. Those blocks weighed me down almost to the breaking point. I can't count the number of trips we made to the basalt factory in Napa. Each load was marked to be cut at a 120 degree angle, or a 90 degree angle or a 45 degree angle. Why the house wasn't designed as a nice little rectangle, which would have been easier on them and me, I don't know. But, when I hear the lavish praise about the flow of space, the attention to view, sun and the northeast winds, I know that even if costly in time and money, all those angles made a great deal of sense both aesthetically and practically.

I was extremely anxious when Elaine went all the way to Novato to get a bargain on doors. Imagine tying six doors on the top of my little frame and driving through traffic and the freeways without placing a red flag where the load stuck over the back of my car! I know she was as concerned as I about the ungainly cargo. We both were grateful we weren't stopped by the Highway Patrol as she crept along, confounding drivers. Happily, we came out of that harrowing experience unscathed.

The trips we made to San Jose were the best. She always was thrilled to be going to Stonelight, her little handmade tile company. While I sweltered in the sizzling valley sun, she spent an inordinate amount of time selecting tiles from their bone pile. She overloaded me with hundreds of the most beautiful green tiles shot through with copper. I didn't mind, as she sang all the way back to Berkeley and couldn't wait to show Henry how varied they were from the different firings. She would regale him with the great discount she had gotten on those tiles that had been rejected because of that very diversity, which she insisted made them all the more beautiful. I must say every time we went down to the factory we were exhilarated, and when we returned she would brag to everyone about her great finds.

That was not so, when we made our trips to the Sinclair Paint Company in San Francisco. She hated those trips and I did too. With all the paint stores in Berkeley and Oakland, I wondered why Bob Stevens had to select a company that was so inaccessible. However, he was wedded to Sinclair for the quality of their paint and their ability to mix colors to his specification. Elaine would order gallons of paint, but never enough, or the wrong color, or she would forget brushes, and back we would go. She never complained, but my tires were wearing thin and I blamed that on those endless trips across the Bay.

And then there were countless trips to the plumbing supply store for long pipes which were tied across my frame, and to the hardware store for nails and to the rental library for tools. I didn't mind those excursions because I knew how important my job was and I enjoyed the camaraderie, and I think that's the way Elaine felt, too.

The only time I remember Elaine complaining bitterly was after pouring the terrace. She exclaimed that edging was a worse job than striking the joints of Henry's concrete block walls. She revived quickly as we headed up to Tahoe after finishing the cement work. I was fitted out with an icebox, sleeping bags, fishing gear and food. We had a *great time, even went to the gaming tables in Reno, which was our downfall. Henry had no stomach for the one-armed bandits, but Elaine lost what little money they had brought. This could have been a disaster in 100 degree heat, as we all were parched and dehydrated when we reached Sacramento on the way home. Luckily, they had enough change to share one orange juice and they filled my radiator with water.*

My good times seemed to be over when they moved into their home in 1950. That's when Henry exchanged his old Cadillac for a brand new white convertible Dodge. Without me, alas, they headed east with their 16mm camera to show off their finished product to Elaine's folks. I admit I was jealous and hurt that they didn't have faith in me to make the trip this time. After all I had done for them, they put me out to pasture. Still, in what I thought was my retirement, I looked pretty snappy in my newly recovered seat covers made from a green awning. I think I graced the parking lot, too.

It seemed in no time, all four McGee children came along in just that many years, and claimed me for their very own. When they outgrew me, I admit I was in a depressed and dilapidated state. Fortunately, I got a new lease on life when Henry hauled me to King Junior High School and I was made much over by the students in the auto mechanics class. So, all in all, I think I've had a pretty rich and varied life with Elaine and Henry, who were workaholics when it came to building their home. But then, I was proud to be their beast of burden.

Throwing the Mud

And now I must get back to the job of building. From the sugar cube houses our architect designed as a kid and from his study of Frank Lloyd Wright's Usonian houses, it was an easy transition for Bob to determine to use basalt block for our home. I found the very thought of a block house distasteful. All I visualized were the ugly rectangular blocks used in commercial buildings along the highway. However, instead of the eight-inch block, Bob ordered the four-inch, which was manufactured in nearby Napa. He assured us that he would achieve warmth with color and the texture of the exposed block. Little did we know then that Bob's genius was to use ordinary materials to create works of art. He'd even painted mundane egg crates and used them as valences to enhance his draperies in his magnificent penthouse apartment in Hollywood.

It became my job, after Henry laid the block, to make certain the vertical joints were flush and to strike the horizontal joints. Using a block of wood with a protruding nail to achieve this effect was a painful experience, like scraping my fingernail against the blackboard all day long; but, should I survive that ordeal, a spectacular shadow detail would be added to the rough texture and color of the block. I thought I performed this task admirably, until one day a few years later, in the middle of a kiss, Henry's eye caught sight of a small hole going right through to the outside. I hasten to add that our final product represented Henry's perfectionist touch rather than mine.

In preparation for the block job we went down the hill to observe a mason at work and to pick his brains. We quickly learned that we were not looked upon as journeymen. Rudely, we were told to step aside as the mason flung mud from his trowel in our direction. He had no interest in divulging the secrets of his trade. Masonry was a hard and closed system. Nevertheless, we became masons. I use 'we' editorially, as my fervent wish during our entire building adventure was to lay even one block. But alas, I was never promoted from hod carrier to mason. Henry had no difficulty carrying on the mason's hierarchical tradition.

Our next step was Sears. There we were intrigued with a gadget called a 'whirl barrel.' The barrel was mounted in such a way that it could be twirled to mix cement, sand and water, then secured and wheeled wherever it was needed. Not long after the whirl barrel was in operation, I could see it serving even more efficiently as a mixer of champagne punch for our housewarming.

After investing in our whirl barrel cement mixer, we frugally bought a few tools we needed to build our block house. We purchased a large and small trowel, a four foot and a two foot level, a good hammer and a hole digger, a real wheel barrel, a hand saw, and later, for framing, we borrowed a skill saw from a friend. That was foolish economy, because we ended up buying him a new one after we finished our job. If we needed a special tool, we would run down to the Berkeley Tool Library and sign for one.

Henry started laying the block in the closet in the back bedroom. We figured little damage could be done in that obscure corner. I stood ready with the family's 35mm camera as he fussed with the block. It took a good twenty minutes while he handled it as though it were a wild beast. First, he tried to butter the cement mixture onto the bottom and sides of the block. Then, he placed it on the wall and tapped it down with a trowel. Finally, he leveled the block and cleaned it. One week later he was at the end of a straight, level wall, four feet high; and now, Henry worked so efficiently and competently, he looked as though he had never done anything else for a living but lay block.

That's not to say the same for his partner. I paid a heavy price as his hod carrier. My job was more or less like mixing ingredients for a cake. To two buckets of cement, which I slung into the barrel as the fine cement dust came flying back into my face, I added three buckets of sand and enough water to give it proper consistency, not too slurry, nor too thick. Then I twirled the mixture, wheeled and dumped it at the feet of the mason. That's what I did all day, every day, that long hot summer of '49. All the while I was getting more and more cement dust in my nose, hair, everywhere. This process was interrupted only by having to tote blocks for Pharaoh's mason. I still sport bulging upper arm muscles after fifty years.

The vignette I just described is pretty much the way our building project evolved. Henry, with his remarkable kinesthetic sense, was able to take on any role required of him. First he would learn the skill, then perfect it, and finally relish it to the fullest. His recurring nightmare was that our former goldbricking contractor would come to him and say he had finished the job and give him the keys. For Henry, participating fully in the process of building was everything.

I was of another stripe. I can't think of a single job I enjoyed other than laying tile. I hated the striking of the joints, the cement dust, the lugging of blocks, the sticky, gritty cold sensation of stuff I had to put on my finger to cover nail heads. My gratification was to stand in the middle of what appeared to be the ruins of Rome and squint to imagine the walls up to grade, thus skipping all the drudgery in between. That's not to say I didn't yearn to have the same joy in the process that Henry had. However, for me, the end result was all, and the sooner the better.

After we finished the back wall I thought we would sail right along. I didn't know then that much of the beauty and stability of Bob's design was due to great piers at the many angles of the house. Each pier used as much block as a twelve-foot wall. Then there were the offsets that took time and more block than a straight wall. It occurred to me that we would save money and time and I could avoid breathing cement dust if we cut out a few of those mighty piers. Of course that would make our home resemble any ordinary block home. Fortunately, I had too much respect for Bob's design to suggest scrimping on his creation.

1949 -- The master of masonry – 1992

1949 -- Striking the joints – 1992

Time was running out and the walls were only halfway up around the house. We desperately wanted to have the walls to height by the end of summer; so when Mac, who delivered our block, mentioned he had seen a masterful mason finishing a non-union job in the hills, we asked him to relay an SOS.

Higginbotham, et al

I shall never forget a giant of a man sauntering onto our slab and tripping over my whirl barrel. Henry explained how I supplied him with mortar and assured him I would supply the mud for him. At that Higginbotham bellowed, "Junk that toy and get me a large electric mixer up here and plenty of cement and sand."

Even though we had intended to build our home entirely with our own hands, we gladly welcomed Higginbotham into our lives. Higginbotham was to become our legendary hero. He was the one who demolished my husband's wall with a withering glance, as Henry put his thumb-bob against his four-foot block wall and proudly challenged him to build one as straight. With his contemptuous reply, Higginbotham boomed, "You make it easy for me. I'll have your wall, as well as your massive chimney, up to grade in less than two weeks." True to his word, he finished in ten days. Had it been one more day, I wouldn't have survived to tell the tale.

Higginbotham was an original, beholden to no one, especially not to the Mason's Union, nor to his wife, who had him put in jail for drunkenness the first night after he had worked for us. He worked hard and fast and lived just as hard and fast. He named his own price and was contemptuous of the walls it took us all summer to get up to four feet. From him we learned that a skilled mason is the pinnacle in his profession. We were mere peons who existed just to serve him. We would arrive on the job at 6 a.m. to start toting blocks, to mix cement and to set up the scaffolding. Higginbotham would arrive at 7:30, hop on the scaffolding and start buttering and laying blocks. No matter how hard I struggled to help Henry move the scaffolding, deliver blocks or furnish the mud, Higginbotham would stand perched above us, smoking a cigarette, never deigning to lift a finger to assist us in our lowly labors. He would stop exactly at five, light a cigarette, drink a can of beer and leave with instructions to have everything in readiness for him the next morning.

After he left, our work would begin in earnest. I would have to finish striking the horizontal joints. Henry would have to clean the tools, the wheel barrel, the cement mixer and start setting up for the next day. We were so beat by the time we finished cleaning up, we would go back to our digs, eat some corn flakes and fall into bed, only to jump up at five to start the marathon all over again.

To see the walls and piers that we had struggled all summer to get up to four feet, rise to eight feet was so exhilarating, we slaved willingly. No matter that our hands were scraped raw, our backs were breaking from the strain of lifting blocks, that we were choking from cement dust and exhausted from too little sleep and a skimpy diet, we carried on, never complaining, not even to each other.

Then fate stepped in to save us from this death struggle. Higginbotham, while jumping from one scaffold to another, slipped and sprained his knee badly. Any normal human would have been out of commission for a week. Not our hero. He wrapped his knee in an Ace bandage and kept on working. However, the sprain slowed him down just enough to set a pace that we could handle.

It wasn't until the last day, when the walls were up to grade and the massive chimney completed, that Higginbotham surveyed the job and became enamored of his handiwork. I can see him leaning against an impressive front pier sneering, "Would you take a hundred thousand dollars for this house?" This was the house that we were building for ten thousand dollars! I still hear my husband's response, "Nothing but the gravest calamity could drive us from this place."

And there were to be many natural calamities that threatened us through the years: landslides in the fifties and sixties, a fire that stopped at the edge of our property in 1970, the Loma Prieta earthquake in 1989 and finally, the firestorm of 1991. None of these were grave enough to pry us from our perch on the hill!

After our experience with Higginbotham, we came to realize that there were certain areas of expertise that were better handled by plumbing, electrical and roofing craftsmen who had the tools, the materials and the skills. We were also aware that there were times when getting extra help avoided catastrophe, like getting the walls up to grade before school started or putting on the roof before the rains.

Our need to rely on outside help opened up a whole new world to us. The people we came to know in the building trades gave us an extraordinary insight into a way of life that was lived on the brink: dramatic, tough, stressful, but satisfying for its immediate gratification.

One of the perks of this other world was meeting Mr. Hugo Steltor. He was an emaciated little fellow with a caved in chest, a chain smoker who coughed frequently. He worked for the city Sewer Department and dug for us after hours. He would come up at five in the afternoon and barrel down the hill, lickety split, or excavate for a septic tank, or dig whatever trench we needed. No one before or since ever dug like this consumptive fellow. After two hours of steady digging, following eight hours of digging for the city, he would stop, put on his tattered jacket, smoke a cigarette and accept a beer. He was so dignified and took such pride in his work that we never were able to call him anything but Mr. Steltor. He did every bit of digging for us for years. Twenty-three years later, after he had retired from the Sewer Department, he dug around a mighty oak in our canyon and saved its life.

One day we were desperate to pour the back bedroom wall. I cajoled a mason plucked from the yellow pages to come up on a Saturday to help us. He consented if he could bring his children. I warmly welcomed him with what turned out to be nine kids who needed breakfast, playtime and lunch.

Another time an electrician asked if he could bring his girlfriend. She came at noon, all dressed up, and visited with us. Then they undressed, sat in the sun and picnicked. They spent the rest of the lunch hour trying to convince us that we should join their nudist colony.

Often, a German professor who had survived the 1923 conflagration in the Berkeley hills would visit us. He was enthusiastic about our block home, which he felt would withstand fire, and egged us on with much encouragement. One day he arrived as Higginbotham was helping Henry hoist forty-foot rafters onto our roof. If it hadn't been for Higginbotham, we would have had to hire a derrick. Our professor exploded in broken German, "Don't you know those timbers will burn when the next fire sweeps through these hills?" We realized he thought our whole house would be made of fireproof materials. He left in disgust and never came back.

Every spare moment we worked on our house. Christmas Day of 1949 we were pounding nails on the roof to the sound of Beethoven's Pastoral. A couple hiking in the hills was so touched by our dedication they scurried home and returned with a festive basket of goodies. Ever after on Christmas day, we were warmed by that remembrance and Beethoven's Pastoral.

There were times when we were naïve to a fault. The day the cement workers poured our slab, we were mesmerized by their hard work. We watched them pile onto their truck all their equipment including our tools and wheel barrel. It wasn't until much later that we realized this was the second time we allowed cement workers to squirrel away our much needed tools.

December 31st of 1949 was brutal, cold, windy and wet. It was that day our electrician decided to bring his whole crew up to the job. The men spent eight hours trying to board the open spaces with plywood. We watched this phenomenon without saying anything and then wrote checks for ten men who had done nothing but try to keep warm.

Don't think we were always such pushovers. Later on I intend to brag about our used timbers, our second hand plate glass windows and our seconds in handmade tile. In some ways, we made out like bandits.

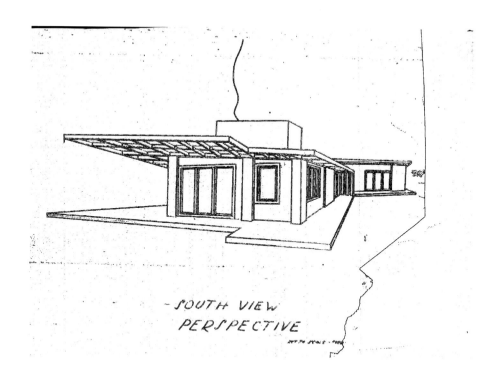

- SOUTH VIEW
PERSPECTIVE

Building Materials

I never graduated from hod carrier to mason, a sad commentary on my husband's lack of faith in my kinesthetic ability. But while Henry was focused on building, I had complete control of fetching materials for him. This was a happy arrangement as we were both doing what we did best.

When we started our building project, we were thinking minimum costs for materials. However, as we were doing everything ourselves, we figured we could splurge, here and there, on copper gutters and kiln-dried four by four redwood mullions. And somehow we ended up with maximum quality and three dollars left over from our $10,000. How we achieved that end, I don't know. I didn't pour over catalogs or choose materials to fit our budget. The fact is I'm not quite sure what I did, but I did stumble upon some good buys.

One day, for example, I happened by an old church that was being torn down. There on the ground were kiln-dried rafters, at least forty feet long, piled on the sidewalk. Until that moment, we had resigned ourselves to renting a derrick, at great cost, to lift iron beams to accommodate our forty-foot spans. I talked to the wreckers and asked to buy the lumber right then and there. It was necessary, they said, to go to the lumberyard to make arrangements.

My elation was dampened when Henry told me the outfit I was dealing with had an unsavory reputation. Armed with that knowledge, I was determined we weren't going to be taken. Every time they threw a rafter on the truck, I would examine it and, if I saw a notch, insist that the board feet I was being charged be reduced to that point. I probably got fifty percent more board feet than I paid for, outfoxing the foxes. That fortuitous find saved us thousands.

In those days, in spite of poor insulation, windowpane was used in most houses as plate glass was too costly. With our tremendous areas of glass, we knew we needed plate but couldn't afford it. Scrounging around a wrecking yard, I found large sections of heavy plate glass taken from store windows as it had been scratched or damaged in some way. Since we needed three by eight foot sections, I was able to salvage enough unblemished pieces, cut to size, to do all of our glass. Once again, we got top quality for less; in this case, plate glass for the price of ordinary windowpane glass.

Along the way, we developed a love affair with railroad ties. Wherever we spotted them, we would pursue the owner. It became such an addiction, we would get excited, even on a trip to Los Angeles, when we saw some ties beside the road two hundred miles from home. To this day, when I see railroad ties lying around unused, I get that same skidding sensation that I experienced as a kid when the first snow fell and we were sent home from school early.

Driving along the bay one day, I noticed a railroad yard with great stacks of railroad ties. After a bit of research, I found that the Southern Pacific had pulled them up from their tracks to be replaced. They would be quite willing to give them to us, just for the taking. Down we went with a rental truck, Henry on the heavy end and me on the other end, while the workers stood around gawking as they watched a little gal helping to heave heavy ten-foot ties onto a rented truck. We came back for many more loads. With those ties we designed a glorious walkway, reminding me of a movement in a Beethoven sonata, with its great platforms and gentle treads snaking down the hill and over the canyon.

One afternoon, Henry tied a rope around me and one around himself, attaching two railroad ties to the other end of the rope. I had no idea what he had in mind, as I started walking in one direction and he went in another. At that moment he roared, "Not that way!" belatedly adding, "Sweet." Only then did I realize we were the oxen chosen to level some rough spots on our property that the bulldozer had neglected. Some bystanders on the road above us happened to be looking down and were ready to report to the police that a guy was abusing his wife. Happily for us, they accepted Henry's explanation and became so enamored of our project that they followed it to its completion. That same couple told us we were making a mistake to build while prices were so high and that they intended to wait. Fifty years later, we dined in their rented apartment.

My favorite find was our handmade tile, which I cherished as our family jewels, along with the lights of the Bay Bridge. Our architect had used the little

Stonelight factory in San Jose for the tiles in his grandmother's kitchen with which I was so smitten. They were extremely costly and we needed great quantities, totally beyond our budget.

Browsing around their yard, I found what was called their 'bone pile' - rejects, in other words. Miraculously, I found great quantities of 'our' tile among the stacks. I hastily inquired about them and was told a woman in Piedmont had ordered them. She didn't appreciate the variation in the handmade tiles, which is the very quality that accounts for their beauty, and had returned them, which accounted for our good luck. I immediately contracted for all of her rejects. That's how our home was loaded with jade and copper for the cost of ordinary tile.

Tile setting is an extremely costly operation, and handmade tile setting is even more so, as it is irregular compared to commercial tile. We received three bids in the thousands of dollars, even though we were supplying the tile. Those bids triggered another research job.

After watching tile setters at work, we rented a tile cutter machine, purchased the proper amount of sand and cement, and proceeded to lay tile on the flat surface of our fireplace ledge. First we laid down a thick coat of cement, then we embedded each tile on that base, carefully spaced and selected for color and variation, and finally we slurped a mixture of runny cement and sand over the entire surface. When we felt the cement had set up sufficiently, we wiped off the mixture, and *voila,* the job was done.

In a few hours we had tiled the seating ledge around the fireplace and the twelve-foot span over the bookshelves in the living room. That afternoon was like child's play and fun, and besides we saved great sums of money. Of course, we didn't stop there. We laid the tile throughout the kitchen, doing all the counters and even the windowsills.

Henry and I never were so focused as when we were in the process of building our home, not even when I primed for my Masters or when Henry took his orals. During the year we spent building, our focus on the house was constant and intense, with no let up. When we were involved with window frames, or with the covering of our roof, or with kitchen pulls, nothing else had any reality for us. Such intense concentration made our hum-drum building routine exciting and often dramatic, as when we spotted a copper roof we just had to have, only to find we couldn't afford it.

First it was the railroad ties, and now it was ceilings. In Pasadena we visited an architect friend and his wife, who had just designed a beautiful new home. We were so enamored of their textured ceilings we talked of nothing else. I hope we were good enough friends so our boorish manners were forgiven. In any case, we came away with the formula and process for achieving the ceilings we wanted.

We drove around for months looking at fascias, the wood covering the end of our roof rafters, and didn't see any that were appropriate. Most houses used narrow trim that would never do for our substantial structure. Bob came up with the answer by using our 2 x 14 inch roofing timbers that were suitable and added to the feeling of strength and stability of our home.

We looked and looked at the barriers people use to protect their privacy and property. You would think observing other people's fences would be a boring way to pass what little spare time we had, but no. We were fascinated by our discoveries, even though so many were downright ugly. In the end, Bob Royston, our landscape architect friend, designed fences for us that were original, functional, aesthetically pleasing, and more trouble to build than most, but worth it.

The kids in front of a section of Royston's fence

Our concrete terrace around the house was of great concern to us. Concrete can be glary, especially on the western side of the house. We

47

flirted with the colored concrete Frank Lloyd Wright used inside his houses, but decided it might not be practical outside. One day, we came upon a finish that exposed the colorful pebbles which was exactly what we wanted. After researching the process, we found it was just a matter of hosing the cement at the proper moment before it set up. We were delighted with the results of that treatment.

But enough about the big problems we decided together. My job was to expedite and select such things as doors, hardware, and appliances. After all, Henry was busy on the job from sunup to sundown. Although I was his inept but passionate assistant in the work area, I became a tiger when it came to choosing the right water heater, or the elegant front door handle.

Such a selective process took its toll on me. Henry could put a level on his wall and know exactly what he must do. I, on the other hand, could look at seven different models of toilets, all with special characteristics to recommend them, and then make a choice based on aesthetics, cost, durability, and even sound. I had always considered inanimate objects simple and uncomplicated. Now I found that each faucet, every towel holder and soap dish assumed a major role in this drama we were producing. That's how I came to select a Case toilet for the master bedroom. The choice was extravagant, but the Case was extremely quiet and its lines so regal that I succumbed. Fortunately, when I was too intemperate in one area, I often could make up for my lavishness in another.

For two folks who shopped for clothes at the thrift store and subsisted on bargain bananas from the Safeway next door, we were painfully choosy about everything we permitted to be a part of our home. My mother scolded us for being so persnickety about our house while dressing like ragamuffins most of the time. Looking back, it does seem remarkable to me that we could have been so single-minded and uncompromising about our choices for our home and so oblivious to all else in our lives.

Take hardware, for example. We knew we didn't want shiny brass or aluminum: only pewter would do. And we knew we didn't want a fancy or elaborate design and that whatever we chose must be carried out throughout the house. Unfortunately, our Cadillac taste didn't jibe with the moderate priced catalogs. Nevertheless, after searching and searching, I did come up with a line I could live with, within our price range, thanks to Mr. Simon of the Simon Hardware Store in Walnut Creek, who special-ordered for me.

That same laborious process was repeated over and over. I found that what was suitable for our home was the key, and that rarely meant it had to be the standard or the most expensive choice. When Bob Stevens suggested that we use etched plywood for our cabinets, I rebelled. The texture seemed too busy for me. He then came up with combed plywood, the stuff they were using to cover walls in five and tens and cheap restaurants. Of course, it became anything but cheap when our cabinetmaker had to meld it onto plain plywood.

However, when we hung the doors flush and painted the cabinets the moss green color used throughout the house, they looked rich and complemented the texture and color of our block walls.

But now I was faced with finding the appropriate hardware. Bob insisted on very expensive piano hinges for the cabinetry. Try as I might and no matter the cost, I couldn't find pulls that complimented those cabinets. After a long and fruitless search, the elegant solution involved a magnetic touch system with no pulls at all.

When we decided to put our refrigerator into a five-foot nook before entering the kitchen, we began to look for larger sizes. One day I saw an advertisement for Col-Temp, a commercial box that was the right dimension. Alas, it looked like what it was, a stainless steel commercial refrigerator. But oh, it was wonderful, especially since up to that time I had functioned with a tiny icebox. It had ten cubic feet of freezer space and twelve cubic feet of refrigerator space, side by side. Bob suggested we have it painted the color of our walls. Appliances, at that time, only came in white or stainless. As I recall, the manufacturer had the color baked on for us, a first for his company. It became a talking point of our home. When we threw our first party, I was able to put a huge plastic dome of an airplane turret full of melon balls on one shelf.

When we needed book shelving, I looked for the proper shelves to span the fourteen-foot ledge under the windows on the east side of the living room. Standard bookshelves looked puny and ineffective. Again Bob came up with the idea of using our rough two by fourteen roofing timbers, which were massive enough to span the area, and when painted out, were smooth and in good scale.

The tile setters told us that our beautiful hand-made tiles were too irregular to set in a shower. Utter nonsense! But unfortunately, we didn't know any better at that time. And so I found a copper-colored commercial tile that was merely adequate. We paid as much for that tile as we did for our gorgeous handmade rejects.

Enough. Under the tutelage of an original like Bob Stevens, I was learning how to select materials that were appropriate and would last a lifetime. It took patience, energy, lots of time and imagination. And so our contemporary home, even after four decades, retained a timeless quality that made people think it had just been built.

Henry and Elaine show off their unique home. From a 1950 Oakland Herald Tribune article and photo spread.

Battles of the Triumvirate

It has been said that if a couple stays together after building a house, nothing can tear them asunder. We learned a great deal about each other and our strongly held priorities. That includes Bob, our architect, who completed the triumvirate. The mosaic of second choices we all were forced to make to accommodate each other may have been why our home turned out to be so special and unique.

I remember trying to avoid a miscarriage in the servant's quarters of the Black Estate, which we were renting, and arriving two weeks later on our building site. Bob and Henry were pouring the last of the cement around the fireplace. I was aghast to see that they had made the ledge on the living room side six inches wider than on the dining side, which seemed to me to unbalance the seating ledge around the fire pit.

"This can't be!" I screamed. It was a Herculean task to break up all the concrete and start over again. I'm sure with each stroke of the axe, Henry and Bob were wishing it were my head. In the end there was no contest. They agreed it had to be done.

While setting the twelve-foot long counter in the kitchen, Henry asked me how I liked the angle. I liked it a lot. He immediately secured the cabinet into the cement floor, which took the whole afternoon. The next day he announced that the angle wasn't right. We were planning to put the refrigerator in that corner, which meant I would have to squeeze through a narrow opening with groceries. That was unacceptable to Henry.

Since I was getting itchy about finishing the job, I insisted that I wouldn't mind pressing through the narrow passageway; in fact, I would rather do so than go two steps back every day. At that point, Henry asked me to run down to the hardware store for some nuts and bolts.

When I returned, the cabinet had been removed and was free standing, ready to be secured once again at the proper angle. It so happened we placed the refrigerator in another alcove, and could have left the counter as it was. However, we were able to make use of that space for a massive butcher block, so all ended well.

Bob had such a sense of flow, space and color, it was sacrilege to challenge him about his overall plan. But I had the gall to do just that. One day, as I was reflecting about livable space, I realized that a window would have to go if we were to have a piano against the one solid wall in the living area. Since we had glass sliding doors across the front and side, and windows over the bookshelves, I thought eliminating that window would be a minor alteration. I got my way that time, but Bob pouted for three months about that change.

There were many times when we were flexible enough to change plans in midstream, and we were agreeable, even excited about doing so. I remember looking at our two bathrooms back-to-back and suggesting that the shower in between could serve both. Sliding doors on either side would tend to create privacy and soundproofing at the same time. However, we all giggled at the hilarious complications that might ensue. That shower became one of the focal talking points of our home and only occasionally did it become embarrassing when a straitlaced guest met his hostess in the shower.

Our plans showed a recessed area for our bed. Henry and I realized if we cut the north wall at an angle we could lie in bed and glimpse the new moon over the Golden Gate. Bob was only too glad to redraw our plans to accommodate that change.

Originally, Bob had drawn posts to support our massive fireplace. We wondered if we could have the hood cantilevered instead. Bob was enthusiastic about that idea. We turned to our engineer for the solution. We had to put heavy steel mesh in the bed of the fire pit, reinforcing steel had to be placed vertically and horizontally in every core and the whole structure poured solid. Then we had to build a brace to support it for twenty-one days while the cement cured. When the fireplace was unveiled, it was awesome. We never regretted the expense nor did we doubt its stability even in earthquake country, not even when our engineer friend would inspect it for cracks year after year and quip, in jest, that he was surprised it was still standing.

If I squint I can see us snuggling in sleeping bags in our commodious fireplace pit in 1949, shutting our eyes to the myriad of stars twinkling through the open-air ceiling. How could we bear to close our home to the open sky? In 1950, after we moved in, I can hear my father's booming voice when he first saw our massive fireplace, "You get what you really want in life, if you want it badly enough!" He was remembering how much his daughter had wanted a real fire in the fake Italian marble fireplace in their family home.

The open fireplace ledge, connecting dining & living rooms

The fight over our mullions (glass door frames) typifies all of our accommodations and compromises. Aluminum frames were the rage, and we thought they would be functional and certainly economical. The very idea of that solution sent Bob into a tailspin. He insisted on four by four, eight foot, kiln-dried redwood mullions to match the four-inch cement block. The redwood was not only frightfully expensive, but no one had made hardware to handle such cumbersome sliding glass doors. Unfortunately, I was obsessed with the need for cross ventilation, especially since we faced the Western sun. Bob stood his ground and said he must have the massive frames, even if it meant we couldn't have sliding doors. I rebelled. That's where Henry's ingenuity came in. He figured how to hang the doors on specially made heavy tracks, and, at the same time, run them on a floor track. He even improvised weather stripping.

The only thing he didn't figure was how to lock those heavy sliding doors. And so we lived in insecure bliss for fourteen years until we rented our house to go on a Fulbright fellowship. And again Henry's ingenuity came to the rescue. He cut one by two pieces of pinewood to fit on top of the off-set tracks, painted them the color of the walls and our renters had the best security on the hill.

Design features: 6 ft. overhang, mullions, lined drapes

There were a few details we didn't quibble about, because we weren't even aware of them. Bob allowed two feet on either side of our ten-foot openings so that draperies would never interfere with our view when they were opened. He also designed a great overhang on the western side, which shielded us until the late afternoon, another stroke of genius that architects totally neglect on our mountain, where most residents have to keep their draperies drawn all day long.

Of course, the beauty and harmony of our home had to do with modules matching. And though no one was conscious that the four-inch modules of the mullions and the four-inch block were the same dimension, the feeling of simplicity and serenity was achieved by just that kind of attention to detail.

To sum up, Bob had to have his say when it came to aesthetics, I had to have my way when it came to lifestyle, and Henry had to make our dream house a reality. Without being aware of it, we had formed a magical combination.

The Triumvirate, four decades later.

House Painting

Bob saw everyone in color. In his lexicon, we were yellow, blue and charcoal. Coming from the desert, doubtless he was influenced by pastel hues. To convince us, he even painted a projection of our home in those colors. We could not be swayed. The problem was not easily solved until he selected the moss green of the lichens, the copper of the monarch butterfly's wings, the sprout green of new leaves in springtime and the charcoal of the oak tree trunks. That color combination satisfied all of us.

One day in 1949, Bob arrived from Los Angeles with the Cadillac of brushes, a four-inch horsehair paintbrush for each of us, along with three paint caps and four five-gallon cans of Toluene paint. This special paint had been used at the 1939 World's Fair for its lasting quality and beauty of color. Bob was so enamored of the product and its ability to transform our drab, basalt block house into a veritable fairy castle, he neglected to tell us that Toluene had been reputed to be dangerous to human health. Had we known the paint was damaging our lungs, we probably would have been reluctant to use it; I, especially, as I did all the painting in the closets and cupboards where there was little ventilation. However, I am still here to tell the tale.

With the first swatch of paint, we all groaned. It was too light. I was sent to the paint store to get lamp black, which Bob proceeded to dump, little by little, into the five-gallon can and stir. I had to make many trips until we finally got it right. But the original formula was so changed that ever after, whenever we painted, we counted on Bob's pure color sense to adjust the formula with lamp black.

The beauty and ease of our paint job was that it took no more skill to paint the block walls than it took Tom Sawyer to whitewash Aunt Polly's fence. That's why I heard Henry, much to my chagrin, bragging to everyone who came on a house tour that his wife found it easier to repaint walls than to dust.

No truer words were ever spoken. When my folks came out to visit, and again when we were preparing for a visit from Kenneth Lindsay, the former Vice Admiral of the British Navy whose seminar I was taking at the University of California, I remember painting the whole house to get rid of the cobwebs. Painting was much easier than dusting the deep grooves that I had struggled to make in our block walls. My parents were impressed with our pristine walls, even if they were bothered by the smell of fresh paint. As for Kenneth, he was so enamored of our home, and that we had built it with our own hands, he wanted to take our story and pictures back to London to show that the youth of America were more than just push button kids.

In progress, fall 1949

Putting on the Lid

During the fall of '49 we spent many a night sleeping in our fireplace pit. With the twinkling firmament, our roof, and Orion and the Big Dipper our comfort, it was painful to contemplate closing ourselves in, but it was inevitable. After a year of arduous construction work, we had to capitulate and put a roof over our heads.

And so, at long last, we were about to spend our first night in our new king size bed, tucked against the north wall which we had angled for the sole purpose of catching the sliver of the new moon over the Golden Gate. Bliss! Or was it? Down the hill came Robert Weaver Stevens, delivering our draperies from Los Angeles. Next morning, I struggled to make breakfast.

Henry left for work, leaving Bob and me to hang eighty-five yards of sprout-colored raw silk. Bob had found the silk material for the unbelievable low price of two dollars a yard, then lined it with flannel to protect the silk and backed it with heavy duty copper-dyed sailcloth. He used the entire basement of the Comstock Towers in Hollywood to hand-stencil the draperies with an oak branch design, again using our distinctive house colors: the charcoal color of oak bark, the moss green of the lichens and the copper of the monarchs. We considered those draperies a masterpiece as well as a structural part of our home. Notwithstanding that they faced the western sun, they remained, over the decades, as true in color as when they were first hung.

The draperies in 1987; backdrop to a mirthful moment celebrating Elaine's parents' 70th wedding anniversary

62

That evening, Henry and Bob sat in the living room sipping sherry. I poured over the Sunset Cook Book, messing up my handmade tile counters with every pot and bowl and ingredient I had, in my struggle to prepare my first dinner in our resplendent kitchen.

Bob had been dismayed when we wrote we would have to recoup our finances before we could afford the magnificent sateen quilt he had selected. That inspired him to use a remnant of the copper sailcloth left over from the lining of our draperies. He then stenciled the same oak leaf motif that was on the draperies and we had a handsome bedspread. Before going to bed, Bob came in to see how Henry liked his handiwork. Henry was delighted. But when Bob began to hand pleat our draperies while we sat on the edge of our bed, and more especially, when Robert Weaver Stevens was handwritten on the bottom of each panel, Henry began to be less appreciative.

Next morning, we were awakened by a knock on the door. "Breakfast is ready and there isn't a single lump in the oatmeal!" The porridge I had cooked the previous morning had been riddled with lumps.

Now that our home was built, Bob began a period of indoctrinating me into the artistry of homemaking. After Henry left for school, Bob and I would get to work. It might take us a whole morning to arrange and hang Revere Ware pots on the fireplace wall, or an entire afternoon to teach me how to make strawberry jam and popovers. Whatever Bob did, he did with a special flair and exquisite perfection, and I was a willing, if bumbling, apprentice. Bob even went so far as to try to make me over. When he wanted me to pile up my hair to better grace the house, I was less than accommodating.

This routine went on for a number of days. Then one evening Henry came home and announced, "We're going to San Francisco for dinner."

"What about Bob?" I asked.

"Bob can take care of himself. He's a big boy. I want you all to myself for once. Besides, it isn't fun playing John's other wife!"

Not long after, Bob left and I had to fend for myself. But Bob had laid an extraordinary foundation for me. He helped me see the possibilities of using materials in original ways, of creating beauty in everyday rituals, but most of all, in teaching me, by example, to behold everything on this earth with childlike wonder. Ours has been a rich and fulfilling relationship for over fifty years. Henry and I are grateful for having had that talented genius, Robert Weaver Stevens, in our lives.

Ode to Robert Weaver Stevens

Filled with glorious color and delicate shadings
A halogen light excites you
The texture of a Burberry rug sends shivers up
your spine
Robins perched on a telephone line
Make spring for you
Satisfying as designing a home
Scrubbing a kitchen grate fulfills as well
Glulams are your current obsession
We say they won't work for us
This shatters you
Your creative juices bubble up
Ideas come tumbling out
Ten rejected
You hit bottom
One we like
You reach a new high
Extravagant with your time
Our money no object
With childlike enthusiasm
You draft for hours
No matter the roof doesn't come together
Rafters are suspended in thin air
The design is a fairy tale like none other
We succumb and gladly.

Furnishings

For two people who don't smoke, we were the recipients of nine silent butlers, a silver sugar and creamer set, which I dearly love, a brass dinner bell and sundry other meaningful wedding gifts that no newly married couple should be without. Thus, we lacked everything we needed to set up housekeeping, which afforded us the rare privilege of starting from scratch.

With three dollars left after completing our house, we were blessed with my father's generous wedding check to furnish our place. Of course the draperies which Bob had designed, lined, interlined and hand stenciled would have been enough, had we had nothing else.

Bob insisted that we invest in moss green wool turf carpeting, which, though expensive, served us well for more than twenty-five years. At my request for an oversized sofa like the one I remembered in my family's home, he designed and had built by his master furniture maker a three-piece sofa, covered with Mr. Prentice's finest upholstery. It was too deep for proper sitting; my fault entirely, as I had insisted on the dimensions, but it was great for lounging. This took care of the living area and provided versatility, as the pieces could be put together or pushed apart as the occasion demanded. He ordered from Mr. Woodson, his special bed maker, a hand-tied king size mattress, and twins for the guest room.

Henry and I were so enamored of our spacious, flowing, moss green, copper and sprout colored home with touches of charcoal, we felt anything more would be redundant, especially since so much was built in. But Bob wasn't satisfied until he sent us from Los Angeles the largest pottery containers ever made to dress up the outside.

Now, all we needed, according to Bob, was an Electrolux vacuum cleaner, a set of Revere Ware pots and some dishes. With a wedding gift from my father's best friend, Bob purchased dishes from a company called Albert of Georgia. This cheap pottery was so handsome we never bought another set. We used it for over four decades and for all occasions; for every day, for all four babies, for entertaining and for picnicking. Years later, when we needed to replace those dishes, we felt compelled to make a special trip to track down Albert. But alas, he had vanished from Georgia and from the face of the earth. I still look in Goodwill and the Salvation Army, hoping some day to find some remnant pieces.

For a chap who was used to designing luxurious sets for movies and glamorous homes for Hollywood celebrities, it must have been painful for Bob to limit his extravagant impulses. Nevertheless, he was able to make our place look splendid, with his magnificent draperies, his moss green rugs and the custom sofa and beds. I was fortunate to find a fragment of a letter Bob sent us about our sofa material, and two pages listing our furnishings and their costs. It reveals a great deal about Bob; how deeply he cared, how original he was even when it came to spelling and how he furnished our home simply, frugally and elegantly within our budget.

Thirteen

Wednesday
May 16, 1950

Dear Henry & Elaine,

I'm rather excited today for several reasons and I feel ready to give you all that I have gathered in ideas and material things for your wonderful home.

First, I want to keep the draperies a secret so am bound to hold back on detail there, but I will cut loose and tell soon!

Now for the main thing — I'm ready to announce that I have utterly exhausted myself eliminating every fabric possible for our wonderful sofa except #233, our original baby — Prentice with my insistance made up a small pillow in down of the Hill fabric, the one Henry liked, and it refused to breathe or come back! It also curled while sewing and was really too

68

I have tried several others and have found they were bad breathers or much too harsh for human skin — so here is my answer - the sample of #233 we have so long played with has never been tendered when this fabric tto is finished at the dye house, it is a lot flatter - check the roll at Malls and Malcolnis, and thusly gives a more continuous texture and does not and will not be too lush for your home — besides it has passed all the tests and Prentice believes that there is no finer fabric to do our job. It is the only fabric with a texture that has passed the finger picking operation! Also its good qualities of cottons will tell the true tale when in use. Please give me the go ahead signal as we are ready for dying and the lining must match the sofa.

Mr. and Mrs. Henry McGee
1350 Grand View Drive
Berkeley 5, Calif.

BASIC DECORATING ITEMS	COST	McGEE DOWN PAYMENTS MADE	TO DATE RECEIPTED PAYMENTS BY STEVENS
* Lighting fixtures from General Lighting Co.	$ 178.45	$ 178.45	$ 178.45
$1.75 difference between painted and unpainted 8-R-40 fixtures - - - - - - - - -	14.00	14.00	14.00
Paint: Elite Glass & Paint Co. Invoice #D8097 - - - - - - - - - - - - -	18.40	18.40	18.40
Paint: Elite Glass & Paint Co. Invoice #D8192 - - - - - - - - - - - - -	200.96	200.96	200.96
Drapery Fabric from Acquavella Textile Co. & Pindler & Pindler Co.			
84.5 yrds. sprout @ 1.50 - - - - - - - -	126.75		126.75
50 yrds. maroon @ 1.50 - - - - - - - - -	75.00		75.00
125 yrds. sail cloth lining @.70 - - -	87.50		87.50
* 50 yrds. dyed oak rust - - - - - - - - -	22.65		22.65
* 125 yrds. vat dyed oak rust @.40 - - -	50.00	250.00	50.00
* Labor draperies & interlining & track painted to color			
Living room- - - - - - - - - - - - - - -	278.92		
Dining room- - - - - - - - - - - - - - -	69.30		
Master bedroom - - - - - - - - - - - - -	107.49		
Child's bedroom- - - - - - - - - - - - -	96.79		
Difference using heavier lining- - - -	30.00	275.00	275.00
4 square pillows - - - - - - - - - - - -	24.00	331.30	331.50
Beds:			
1 king size 6' x 7' - - - - - - - - - - - -	100.00		
2 single Hollywood beds—each 52.50 - - -	105.00		
12 legs - 6 for each- - - - - - - - - - - -	8.00	100.00	100.00
3 pads for beds - - - - - - - - - - - - -	11.80	130.80	124.80
* Hand blocking of sprout draperies- - - - - -	150.00	150.00	150.00

	COST	McGEE DOWN PAYMENTS MADE	TO DATE RECEIPTED PAYMENTS BY STEVENS
One custom sofa designed by Stevens in 3 parts down loose pillow back & foam & spring cushions - - - - - - - - - - - - - -	575.00	200.00 375.00	200.00 375.00
30 yds. metallic textured fabric #233 at 8.00 a yd.- - - - - - - - - - - - - - - - -	240.00	240.00	240.00
* 30 yds. dyed rust at .75 a yd. - - - - - - -	22.50	22.50	22.50
* Asphalt tile - Sears Bros. - - - - - - - - -	252.67	252.67	252.67
* Bed Throw (Labor only) - - - - - - - - - - -	18.18		18.18
2 terra-cotta terrace pots - - - - - - - - -	32.80		32.80
November Down Payment- - - - - - - - - - - - -		261.00	
TOTALS - - - - - - - - - - - - - - - - - - -	2896.16	3000.08	2896.16
DECORATOR'S 10% - - - - - - - - - - - - - -	289.62	150.00 25.27 100.00	289.62
DECORATOR'S 10% of Carpeting (Listed Below)	63.02		63.02
Gift Pottery from Knobler- - - - - - - - - -	54.50	50.00	54.50
T O T A L S - - - - - - - - - - - - - - - - -	3303.30	3325.35	3303.30
3% Sales Tax on taxables - - - - - - - - - -	48.36		
* items non-taxable or tax paid	3351.66		
Subtract Down Payment Column - - -	3325.35		
BALANCE PAYABLE- - - - - - - - - - - - - - -	26.31		

```
            Carpeting:  (Paid Direct)
               61 sq.yds.carpeting at
                   11.50 a sq.yd. - - - - $701.50
                   Less 20%- - - - - - - - -  140.30
                                            561.20
            ADD:  61 sq.yds. padding at
                   1.00 a sq.yd. - - - - - -   61.00
                 * Hand sewing - - - - - - -    8.00
                                             630.20
            Down payment--1949--200.00 -   200.00
                                            430.20
            3% on taxables - - - - - - -     12.67
            Balance Payment Made Direct-   442.87
```

R OBERT WEAVER STEVENS

71

Our Dining Tables

When we first moved into our home, we dined on our fireplace ledge because I couldn't decide just what kind of dining room table I wanted. The informality of sitting on the floor suited me just fine and went along with Henry's idea of casual living, as well.

I even had the audacity to serve dinner on the ledge for our first guest, Stanley Hiller, the local entrepreneur who owned the fifty acres we had flirted with before we found our site. Uncomfortable as he must have been sitting on the floor, he was so smitten with our home that he asked Henry how much he made as a school principal and then offered to quadruple his salary if he would develop homes on his property. But there was no way Henry could bring his passion for building his own home to that of building spec homes. Little did we know then that we would end up building three homes for ourselves, and that I, a left-hander figuratively and literally, would become a designer and builder of tables.

Even in sixth grade, my sewing teacher had the class look at their left-handed classmate trying to sew a hem, only to find that the left-hander had changed to her right hand when sewing a pocket shut on the other side of the apron. The idea that anyone so inept with both hands could design and construct anything was ludicrous. That didn't take into account the influence of my playmates, who were geniuses in their own spheres. Henry showed me that with confidence and intelligence, trial and error, determination and patience, I could accomplish anything, if I wanted it badly enough. Throughout our married life he carried me right along, recognizing that the impossible just took a little longer. As for Robert Weaver Stevens, with his childlike enthusiasms and artistry, he schooled me in the notion that all materials were placed on this earth for our inventive and aesthetic pleasure. Together these chaps expanded my horizon until I began to see extraordinary possibilities in ordinary materials and how to use them creatively.

Our awkward eating arrangement went on for some time, until I saw in the New Yorker a Salterini wrought iron glass-top table, which seemed to be the least offensive table for our dining area. I also ordered a glass top coffee table to match. Childless at the time, I didn't reckon that there would come a time when a daughter would break the glass top in the dining room and a son would break the glass in the living room. Left with well-designed wrought iron frames, I determined we must find a durable solution for our tables. I replaced the top in the dining room with a four by eight piece of 3/4" outdoor plywood and covered it with a beautiful copper colored handmade clay tile from Spain. Experienced by now, I set about redoing the coffee table. Since it was a round table with a planter in the middle, I figured the easiest thing to do was to break the tiles with a hammer and fit them together around the planter, like a jigsaw puzzle.

The Salterini glass-top dining table

Not long after, Henry suggested that we needed a large table for our deck. It never occurred to either of us to buy one. I now was recognized as our official table maker. This gave me the confidence to order a six foot round piece of plywood with a three foot cutout in the center to accommodate a barbeque. Henry fastened some simple wrought iron legs to the plywood and we were in business. I had never seen a table like that, but it made great sense as we could seat twelve people and even keep warm on cooler nights as we barbequed chicken in the center. The table itself was especially pleasing, as I had found some electric blue tiles at my favorite tile factory in San Jose.

As our family grew, we needed a larger dining table. We had grown fond of our round outdoor table so we cut another six foot round. This time, instead of a barbeque, I had a three-foot round plywood piece cut for the center and Henry found some ball bearings on which it could sit. Again, I used a beautiful Spanish clay tile, but I didn't have enough for the turntable. So I selected a slightly darker copper color, and jig-sawed the tile as I had done for the coffee table. This added depth and variety to the large tabletop. I then set it on the Salterini frame.

Elaine's tile dining table and Lazy Susan; copper Revere Ware pots and pans hang by the built-in oven.

It was this table that became a structural part of our life ever after. I loved putting the whole meal on the table to serve my family of six, never having to jump up during the meal. Of course we had to learn to be watchful not to spin the turntable when someone else was taking seconds, but we enjoyed the gracious flow of conversation that a large round table affords.

Except for Henry's Fulbright year in Ceylon in 1964 when our cook Ambrose served us, I was never able to function with a rectangular table again. That led to some interesting adaptations as Henry accepted posts around the world.

When we lived in Rome in 1968, I decided to surprise Henry for his birthday with a round table. At a nearby quarry I spotted a large piece of travertine which I had cut into a six foot round, with enough left over for a three foot round turntable. Two months went by as I tried to find a way to get the marble, which weighed tons, up to our third floor apartment near the Via Cassia. Where were Caesar's legions when I needed them? Finally I found a group of three strong men at the Ponte Milvia who figured how to wrap rope around the marble and hoist it through the window.

Meanwhile, I had driven past a yard where I saw all sorts and sizes of drainage pipe, and was able to select one of suitable height and width. The end result became the talk of Rome, until our physics teacher came to dinner. He sat with his legs to the side of the table as he asked if we had figured the "sheer." He feared we could have our legs cut off when the marble cracked. For a few days we all sat sideways to the table, waiting for his calculations which never came and which we decided to ignore anyway. The table served us and all our expatriate friends in Rome for two years. Doubtless it is still there, as who could move it?

Our next challenge came when Henry became Headmaster at Brent School in the Philippines in 1972. There we inherited a Philippine mahogany round table in the headmaster's cottage, just waiting for us. All I had to do was add a three-foot round turntable that I covered with capice shell, the beautiful shell that looks like mother of pearl. We placed it on ball bearings, which were always a part of our baggage by now. The result was dazzling.

What I remember most about that table is the party we gave for the gold mining executives who had been so kind to us when Marcos instituted the curfew. As Nellie, our maid, pulled the pan from the oven, the roast beef, carrots, potatoes and onions crashed to the floor. Our guests witnessed this catastrophe, as there was no door to the kitchen, but insisted the dinner be picked up and served. I'm convinced that our glamorous table had much to do with their ability to enjoy each mouthful from the floor, though I admit I couldn't eat a bite myself.

When we returned to Berkeley in 1976, all four of our kids were away at school so we decided to reduce the size of our table. This time we tiled two half rounds, which we pushed together, reserving a one foot leaf to add when we wanted a larger table.

Meeting the Neighbors

As the only house on our hill in 1950, I would feel put upon when our privacy was threatened by an occasional stray car that came up to enjoy the view, or when I received an unexpected visit from a plumber while running around nude on our deck. But that's not to say we were devoid of a variety of special neighbors who made life interesting.

Early on, while we were entertaining a San Francisco couple for dinner, we put on a rural floor show when a deer loped gracefully to and fro across our lawn. That same deer so decimated our planting that we called the Alameda County Hospital and were told we were within our rights to rid ourselves of the deer when it was on our property, but we would be responsible for its disposal, as they didn't want it at that time. Our feelings had become jaded after Bambi had eaten every plant, tender or not, even those known to be deer resistant, so we were more than prepared to cope with his demise.

Henry took action with a borrowed rifle of World War I vintage. With the deer carcass in hand, he beseeched me to run quickly to the Elmwood Library to get a book on how to butcher it. The nearest 'how to' example I could find was how to butcher a cow. I can still see Henry with the deer strung up on one of our mighty oaks, book propped in the crotch of the tree, giving it a go. I hadn't the stomach to watch the operation but I'm sure, as with every task Henry took on, it was done with precision.

I hadn't the stomach to eat the beautifully wrapped and frozen deer meat, either. No matter how I marinated and treated the deer, using every fancy recipe I could find, I had to hide my gagging with each mouthful. Henry, on the other hand, relished every bite and was thrilled to think how much money we were saving by not having to purchase beef at the market.

When my family came out to visit us for the first time, my father must have noticed how repulsed I was with the delicacy we were serving, though I tried not to show it. The next night at dinner, my Dad announced, "Sis, I've been wondering what to get you for a house gift, how about a hind quarter of beef?"

After eliminating our most persistent neighbor, we soon acquired others. Henry was intrigued with a scientific article, in which he had read about raising chickens in an elevated coop. Even before finishing our home, he took time out to build what only could be called a chicken palace. However, after buying baby chicks, we realized they would need to live in an incubator for a while before moving into the big house. Every night we would tiptoe into the hall to check on our babies. Pampered as they were, it never occurred to us that they would establish a pecking order. But one night the smallest of the bunch was lying down looking pretty dead. Henry gently picked it up. It was still breathing, but cold. So he popped it into the oven for a moment and, miraculously, it revived. The next night Henry administered the same treatment on another chick but that one didn't survive.

Soon the rest of the sturdy lot were ready to make it on their own in their splendid residence. Not only had they grown into beautiful, mature chickens, but they soon regaled us with two large eggs every day. One night Henry brought me a chicken to cook. When I learned it was one of ours that we had nurtured with such loving care, I lost my appetite. Along with nurturing our chickens, we started an orchard and planted artichokes on the lower level.

Harvesting cherries and artichokes on the lower level.

And then there were the pack rats. I just knew those little beasties were charming little creatures who had a strong sense of fair play. Unfortunately, I never had an opportunity to meet them, though I knew they had visited us. No matter what they took, they always left something in return, a pebble, some moss, a bit of dry weeds.

We also welcomed a little quail family that flitted about on the front lawn. They were monogamous and devoted to their babies. The mother stayed close to her flock while the father perched from afar and guarded his brood. We missed them when they left us, as they invariably did, happily to return every spring.

The blue jays were housed in our oaks and acted as though they owned our trees and us. They screeched and violently shook the leaves of the trees and chased every other bird away, especially the little hummingbirds. While they were handsome to look at, we developed a strong aversion to those aggressive creatures. Not so with the owl who took possession of the large oak at the top of our hill. He devoted his life to us.

We were besieged by oak worms that first year. They hung from the branches, got into everything, and had to be sprayed, at an exorbitant cost. To compensate, an army of magnificent monarch butterflies invaded our property, their orange and black wings a perfect complement to the colors of our home.

Sharing our Home

It has been our greatest pleasure to share our home from the cradle to the grave, first with parents in the University Nursery School and five decades later with the Seniors Memoir Class. But my fantasy of wheeling our whirl barrel full of champagne punch among our friends at an open house was shattered when Henry announced one day, "By the way, I've invited the principals and their wives for our fall get-together." I was stunned. There was no way we could meet that deadline. But the September 25th date did spur us on to finish - almost.

It was the very afternoon of the party that I brought our garbage disposal home. Considering we had been entertaining in our rented tree house with a small icebox and the bathroom sink while we were building, I don't know why I felt we needed to have a disposal functioning to entertain in our brand new house, but I did.

Henry got to work installing it. I stood by to fetch tools for him as he lay prostrate under the sink. We were a greasy couple and barely had time to wash our hands and throw on some clothes when the first guests arrived. All I remember of that affair is what happened after the last guests departed. We kept stuffing coffee grounds into the disposal all evening, delighted that we could get rid of them so efficiently. Little did we know that by packing the grounds in and not putting on the disposal each time, they would make the disposal inoperative.

That episode didn't dampen our spirits. We had entertained a large crowd and within minutes after they left, the place looked as though they had never been there. The ease with which we could manage seemed to be our major goal in entertaining. We were delighted with the way the house accommodated to the ordinary aspects of living. However, for a long time we seemed to get more of a bang out of cleaning up after our friends left than enjoying them while they were with us.

Even before we finished closing in the pool area, Henry invited a hundred kids from West Oakland for a swim and barbeque. To protect the pool area since we hadn't finished constructing the fence, we put up temporary barriers of plywood, which I plastered with colorful posters to jazz up the place a little. Henry threw in some ice cubes as a joke, but that didn't deter those junior high kids from jumping into the freezing water. Building the pool had proved to be almost more of a challenge than building the house, since one of the walls was on the edge of a fifty foot drop into the canyon. Once again, Henry's building skills were equal to the task.

One of my favorite memories was the party we threw to raise money for the 1956 presidential campaign. We were desperate to contribute. When I mentioned casually to my best friend that maybe we could have a fundraising event at our place, we immediately took action. The result was a great jazz band and bar on our deck, which was suspended on its imagination but which held up bravely, supporting a piano and hundreds of dancing feet, only to succumb to an unusually heavy rainy season in 1957. With music resounding throughout the area, people came rushing up, down and over the hills. It was a huge success financially and proved to us that we could offer our home throughout the years as our contribution to causes we believed in.

Family and friends enjoying the pool

To this day I get chills when I think of the dinner we gave for Henry's faculty and their spouses, seventy in all, with a full complement of four babies under four to be fed. As inveterate do-it-yourselfers, it never occurred to either of us to get outside help. Henry set up long planks on sawhorses on the deck to seat seventy people, and I used every spare moment to cut up watermelon, honeydew and cantaloupe balls and slice salad veggies and garlic bread.

The night of the dinner was a gentle moonlit evening, and that was fortunate, as we couldn't have handled that size group inside. I can honestly say that over fifty years, whenever we've hosted a large event, the climate has always cooperated, even in June of 1999 for the wedding for our youngest son. That morning dawned foggy and cold, as it had been for weeks, but I knew that by one o'clock, when the first guests arrived, it would be warm and sunny, truly a Shangri-la.

I am certain the teachers, as they congregated on the deck drinking our poor man's version of Trader Vic's (cheap white wine mixed with limeade), had no notion that I, while feeding my kids in the kitchen, also acted as sole caterer, cook, server and dishwasher. Even Henry had to desert me to play host.

Luckily, we had a huge plastic dome from an airplane turret into which I dumped the spaghetti and then the garlic bread. Again I rushed into the kitchen, washed the dome and mixed the salad in it. After it was empty, I ran back and served the melon balls. Everyone was jolly, as our mixed drink packed quite a wallop, so no one, not even Henry, thought to help. I still feel queasy when I remember that affair; however, that didn't deter us from opening our home for numerous other school related events. Serving scrambled eggs, sausages, English muffins, jam, coffee and juice all at once to thirty educators was easy after that spaghetti dinner, as was a luncheon and fashion show around the pool for the principals' wives club.

When Henry received his doctorate in 1952, I decided to throw him a surprise party, and invited his committee, a very special group, including Elsa Frankel Brunswick and Nevitt Sanford, who had written the "Authoritarian Personality." That was the one time I had an affair catered, as I didn't see how I could prepare dinner and surprise Henry. To get him out of the house, I asked Walter Loban, who was our neighbor and head of his committee, to invite him to his place to discuss editing his thesis for the "Journal of Genetic Psychology." Henry cherished that surprise dinner party all his life.

But above all else, our home became the hub for our entire family. My mother and father would come out twice a year from the East, my brother's family would come up from the South and the rest of us in the Bay Area would gather for all occasions. The warmth and joy we derived from those reunions were and still are worth ten times over the struggle to build our home.

A family gathering, 1984

However, much as we were devoted to our home, and sharing it, our wanderlust lured us away for a number of sabbaticals. Those adventures necessitated renting. Sharing it in this way led to disastrous results. If Earl Warren, who flirted with renting it, had done so in 1968, we would have been saved from having our home rented to a filmmaker associated with the sixties San Francisco rock scene. That communal family, including numerous Great Danes and several motorcycles, occupied our home and stained our custom carpets. The utilities were cut off at one point for lack of payment and they cooked thereafter in the fireplace, which transformed our beautiful moss green walls into a dreary black. Renting turned out to be so painful that Henry flirted with the notion of selling while we were in Rome. Of course we never could, as it would have been over my dead body.

I do know, in our innocence, we had built a home for all ages. While preparing lunch, I could watch our babes pedaling around the front lawn, etched against the Golden Gate. As little children, they and their friends felt a wonderful sense of freedom scampering round and round the cantilevered fireplace, and as teenagers they lounged on the fireplace ledge listening to pop music. As for our guests, they marveled, as did we, at the ease with which our home lent itself for entertaining; as for our parents, they never tired of relaxing in easy chairs with the awe-inspiring panorama of the Bay Area stretched before them.

The Joy of Living

Was it worth it, all the planning, all the labor, all our mistakes, all our highs and all our lows? Did we achieve our goal: to live simply, comfortably and with ease, in a pleasing environment that we could afford? Let me count the ways.

We knew we didn't want help to maintain our home. That's why our design, flowing around the living, dining and kitchen areas, was able to create an inviting, convenient and efficient communal space. And that's why our quarters, separated from the main living area, became a private and restful retreat. That's why the cantilevered fireplace, the core of the house, invites the cook, the diners and those reclining on sofas in the living area to enjoy the massive wood burning fire place, all at the same time. That's why Bob's 'built-ins' simplified our living. His u-shaped piers accepted our television and hi-fi, as well as our storage and guest closets, and allowed for a washer and dryer. That's why he carefully designed a central location for utilities in the structure behind the massive fireplace.

And that's why I can sunbathe in the middle of a sunbeam in the dead of winter with the sliding doors open to the southern exposure. For that matter, that's why we can prance in and out of every room to enjoy a different exposure whenever we choose. With sliding glass doors on all sides of the house allowing for cross ventilation, we have no need for air conditioning, even in the hottest weather. The prevailing western breezes blow flying insects right through and out of our home, so we have no need for screens. The wall dividing the den from our bedroom allows for a television set to swivel from den to bedroom, conveniently hidden by a painting. The long kitchen counter with bar and cabinets, as well as a wall of cabinets in the dining area, take care of everything but the dining table and chairs. Our commodious round dining table with its three-foot Lazy Susan turntable is a great convenience for serving a large family and for entertaining frequent guests. The fact is, with all of our built-ins, we need very few pieces of furniture.

Most homes in the area, facing the western vista, have to draw draperies as protection from the sun. We, because of our large overhang, can enjoy the bay view throughout the day. Our radiant heated floors permit us to run around barefoot even in the coldest weather. Our substantial structure, built of concrete block, eliminates noise, especially during fifty-mile-an-hour winds, and seems to protect us from the sharp earthquakes we experience from time to time.

Perhaps living on a mountain and still having our home sited on one level makes all the difference. This permits easy access for groceries. It allows us to step from our bedroom into the pool and spa. It makes us able to entertain easily, indoors and out.

The flow, the color and the harmonious use of materials in our home go a long way toward making 'just plain living' a joyful experience. Bob's overall design has accommodated us throughout our lives. It was a great house when we were childless and it adapted remarkably well when we had four kiddies in less than four years. 'Cheaper by the Dozen' should have been written about Henry. That's when Bob's design came into play in earnest and aided Henry's ability to make order out of chaos. We could throw four sets of diapers into the washer and dryer, located next to the nursery.

I remember my mother saying that not even the princesses of England could have been attended to with such expeditiousness. The same went for distributing bottles. So efficient was our method, it became our way of life, and we forgot to wean! I well remember a dinner party where I had Suzanne in a jumping jack contraption suspended from the ceiling. At the same time, Diane was being nursed in my arms, Phillip was being rocked in his cradle by Henry, and Paul, in the nursery, was calling for his bottle to be cooled. It was then that I realized if he could demand a different temperature for his bottle, he jolly well didn't need one.

Early on I wanted our kids to socialize, but they would have none of nursery school. They had everything they wanted at home. Even when they went to grammar school, they would trudge up the hill, relieved to get away from the hubbub of the school. They grew up riding their tricycles around the concrete path in the front of the house and getting dunked in the pool for their evening bath, a great way to live for them and easy on their parents. We didn't realize that living more or less isolated on our hill, they grew up like little children from another planet. They were at peace in their mountain retreat.

Viewing our phantom city across the Bay and living so close to our oaks and canyon has made the natural beauty of our surroundings an integral part of our lives. We all are grateful, in this rough and tumble world, that our home has expanded our perspective and has evoked a special kind of peace and serenity in our lives for over four decades.

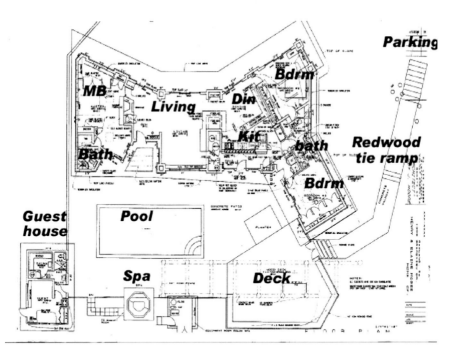

A plan of the original house, showing additions:
pool and master suite (1957);
enlarged deck, guesthouse, sauna, and hot tub (1968).

Paradise Lost

As we ambled down the fairway
Little did we know the blackened sky
Was our home passing by.
We didn't flee the raging flames
Nor rescue family pictures
We weren't overcome by choking smoke
Nor stymied by clogged roadways
We didn't experience the crackling fire
Only the charred remains.
We could only pray and wait
Reclaim our son and daughter
And that made all the difference
With tooth brush and razor
Outside the Marriott next morning
We breathed deeply
No matter we had lost our home
The autumnal sun shimmered on the sea
And for one brief moment
Unencumbered by possessions
We were in ecstasy.

October 20, 1991

Recreating our Paradise

Today, when wildfires rage all over California, I relive what it means to lose a home and everything in it. I shudder to think of the anguish that fire victims endure, as well as the Herculean task that confronts them in rebuilding their homes and lives. I hope our story of rebuilding after the Oakland-Berkeley firestorm of October 1991, when over 3,300 homes burned to the ground, will help others who are facing the same traumatic experience of having lost their homes.

Before and after October 20, 1991

Homeless

Sunday, October 20, 1991, I was reluctant to play golf. The Santa Ana winds were blowing the leaves about the deck and into our pool and the heat was stifling. "Henry," I pleaded, "can't we cancel our golf with the Dubays? I don't want to leave home today. The oppressive heat and these eerie winds are just like those that caused the 1970 fire."

"Of course we'll go. You certainly don't want to hang around for ten days waiting for these Diablo winds to stop blowing."

"Well, hold on. I have to put my ring in the safe." I went into the house and absentmindedly selected a visor instead of putting my mother's emerald ring away.

So, there we were at the Presidio Golf Club in San Francisco, stomping down the sixth fairway, wondering why the sky was so dark and musing that it must be caused by a fire at the Embarcadero. When we reached the seventh hole I asked the Marshal, who was riding around with a little TV set in his cart, what was causing the blackened sky. "Do you remember the Oakland fire of 1970? There's a fire out of control in that same area."

"That area," I stammered, "is where my brother lost his home eleven years ago and I abandoned ours, which was in the direct path of the fire. Sweetheart, let's go home."

"Well, we might as well play in." Henry scored his usual par but I could barely see the ball, let alone hit it.

Driving over the Bay Bridge we could see the flames, and we prayed that our son had gone to the beach as he had intended and wasn't caught in the conflagration. When we arrived at Claremont Avenue, we learned from our neighbor, Steve, who had a poster shop next to the Star Grocery, that no one was allowed to venture up our hill, and that our son had rescued a few people as he drove out over the flames. He had stopped at Steve's store to tell him that Willard Junior High had been designated an emergency fire center. Relieved that he was safe, we called our daughter, Suzanne, in North Berkeley and arranged to meet her at the center, then raced over to the school. We were so grateful when we all got together we didn't even think about the loss of our home and everything we owned.

We commiserated with our neighbors and we all worried about the possibility that some didn't make it, especially one neighbor whom my son had tried to rescue. She refused to go, declaring her home was "fireproof." The next day we were devastated to learn that only her teeth were found.

Looking out from the living room

Sifting through the dining room

Since we had no way of knowing if the wind might shift and engulf Suzanne's digs in North Berkeley as well, we felt fortunate to get one large room for all four of us at the Berkeley Marriott on the waterfront.

Awakening the next morning, how could we explain our feelings on that sparkling clear day with the sun shimmering on the water? We left the hotel carrying all we now owned: two toothbrushes and a razor in a paper bag. No matter how passionate and focused we had been about creating our home, after four decades of good living it didn't owe us anything. For one exquisite moment, we felt unencumbered and liberated from all our possessions and entangling alliances. After all, we had recovered what mattered most: our kids and ourselves.

We didn't sustain that sublime feeling for long. When we tried to find shelter, along with 3,300 other families who were in the same predicament, it was inevitable that choice was limited and rental prices exorbitant. Late in the afternoon I put my head on Henry's shoulders and whined, "I'm tired. Let's go home and look again tomorrow." Only then did the realization that we had no home to go home to hit me and I sobbed uncontrollably.

Watching TV in makeshift quarters that night, I saw Bosnian refugees with no country, no place to be, no loving family or friends to support them, no insurance to help them rebuild. I never whimpered again.

After losing our home, we learned, as in everything else in life, that Henry and I faced trauma in very different ways. Henry didn't waste a moment fretting about the loss of our home that meant so much to him. He even quipped, "What an effective way to get rid of all of our junk!"

His attitude was a welcome counterbalance to mine. My fragility about loss has a painful history. My sense is that nothing I care deeply about ever survives. It was as though I lost my right arm when my folks sold our family home, along with my fifth grade novel, which was stashed in the attic. And now, I was extremely vulnerable about the loss of letters, my stories of Ceylon, the crayon drawing of cats done by my five year old daughter, not to mention the loss of photos, our home movies and my parents' love letters.

When, at last, I was allowed up on our site, I saw that great, once joyous cantilevered fireplace, which was the hub of our home, around which centered the living, dining and food preparation, and I shuddered. Designed to withstand earthquakes, flood and fire, our fireplace still stood proud and commanding, though its surface was blackened and the tiles on the seating ledge were chipped. It resembled a monster tombstone, dwarfing the rubble of forty-one years within its confines. There was no way I could face the fact that it must be demolished. Like the Roman aqueducts, that structure was engineered to last forever, with iron in its base, reinforced in every core and solid with concrete. But the engineers insisted, "Nothing can withstand a firestorm of 2,000 degrees Fahrenheit."

The cantilevered fireplace stillstanding at left

While I was musing on our site, among the ruins one evening, a contractor wandered by. His first words endeared him to me. "People are going wild in this fire area, crushing everything under the bulldozer's blade. You won't have to take down that great structure." That remark gave me the courage to take a stand. "Henry, I have to be convinced before we tear down our fireplace."

Henry took a hammer and banged it against a corner of the cantilever, exposing the reinforcing rod which had pulled away from the cement. I had to admit the structural strength had been compromised. But it took a whole week for the bulldozer to tear it down. I still wonder…

Nevertheless, with Henry by my side, I wasn't permitted to fritter away my time mourning our hearth that would never warm us again. We both fervently wished that we had not lost our home, but with our 'know how' we knew we could replace our material losses, not, perhaps, without a tussle with our insurance company, but replace them just the same. That left us, especially me, to mourn only those things that were irreplaceable.

Still, there was a big price to pay. Our home had developed a soul. That soul was what the whole family missed. Our home had so insinuated itself in our lives that it was impossible to imagine our family without it.

From the beginning, Henry and I had treated our home as our first baby, caring for its every need, buying thrift store clothes so it could be given every advantage. We responded like proud parents as it grew and developed. But gradually, it had matured. Almost without our recognizing what had happened, our home began to assume a different role in the family; that of matriarch, holding us all in its firm embrace.

The loss of our home was hard on our kids, especially Diane and Phillip, who lived away from home. Our other two were so much a part of the process of rebuilding they didn't have time to grieve. Our son Paul, who is a lawyer, helped us with endless conferences with the insurance company. Our daughter, Suzanne, a landscape designer, took photographs of the thirty two trees that had burned and started to transform what had become the McGee mud hole into a park once again. Diane and Phillip visited often, and everyone had an opinion about the design details of the new house.

I recall feeling put upon when expediting for materials. Henry never challenged me in that department when we built our first home, but our kids felt strongly about various aspects of the house and wanted me to incorporate their suggestions. "This is our home, not yours!" I wanted to shout. But then I decided I should be grateful that they cared that much, even when I didn't take their advice.

But, should I be grateful? Could it be that the dreams we had for our children of finding the right partners and establishing their own homes were thwarted by what we had created? To this day, Paul lives in the guest cottage, taking care of the pool, cooking dinner, cleaning house and washing windows, while Suzanne inhabits the guest room and nurtures the lush landscape she has created.

It is comforting and exhilarating to have young people around, but I often wonder if we're caught in a web so seductive it prevents us, especially my kids, from venturing into the outside world.

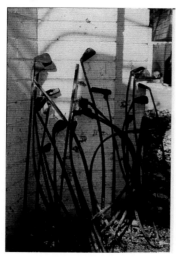

A Refugee's Reverie

Our scene is ever-changing
Like the sea
Never repeating,
San Francisco emerging from the fog.
A sparkling necklace of glittering lights
The family jewels,
Stolen from the Bay Bridge.
The Farallones, etched against the horizon
On a clear December day.
The ominous clouds swirling Alcatraz
Mirroring the charcoal bay, smooth as glass.
The brilliant tapestries
Stretched across the autumnal sky.
And that ball of fire
Setting behind the Golden Gate.

Reflections after the Fire

Even as the embers glowed, like the lemmings or the men of Aran, we knew we had to return. That was not so for many of the families who lost their homes in the fire of 1991. Many left their homes that day and bought elsewhere, even sacrificing a larger insurance settlement had they rebuilt. Three of our closest neighbors died during that stressful period. Some were uncertain about where they wished to settle. A few rebuilt only to put their homes up for sale. Others, like us, struggled with insurance companies, plans, architects and building and are now settled in our rebuilt homes.

I sometimes wonder if much of our married life could have been a preparation for facing up to the trauma of losing our home. After all, we had built it from scratch. That rare experience was one most fire victims hadn't had. And then, living in six different rentals, in six different neighborhoods after the fire, mirrored our earlier experiences as we accommodated to living abroad in Ceylon, the Philippines and Rome with four children. This time it should have been less stressful, since our kids were grown and we had no possessions and no foreign language or currency to deal with. Also, this time the insurance company picked up the tab. However, the anxious years it took to come to a satisfactory settlement with our insurance company and rebuild caused us stress and pain enough to make our homeless state something less enjoyable than a junket abroad.

We camped wherever we could find a furnished place to accommodate us as we rebuilt our home. We were extremely fortunate that our policy covered us generously for rental expenses. The problem was that there were very few rentals available at any price or for any length of time. Luckily, during the first few weeks we had friends who offered us their lovely home in North Berkeley. As they had lived for many years in Kashmir and Pakistan, they were extremely security conscious. We felt like caged animals every time we entered or left the house. The firemen had to come up three times to bail us out because of the ringing of sirens when we neglected to shut off the alarm.

Our next stop was with dear friends whose main house had escaped the fire by inches. They insisted that they would feel less guilty living in their home, since it came out of the fire unscathed, if we would move in with them until we found a suitable place. They had, however, suffered damage to their guest house. As a result, they would meet with a contractor in one room while we worked with our architect in another. It was like a house party when we got together every evening for cocktails. I even remember putting on a fashion show after I had acquired, from my favorite second hand store, a number of stylish outfits to replace my wardrobe.

By now, we determined that we must find a furnished place of our own. We were willing to take short-term rentals, as we had nothing to move but ourselves. When we had to wait to get into the next rental, we went to an Elderhostel. We considered those sojourns 'our home away from home.' When we were at an Elderhostel in San Diego, and again at Indian Wells, Bob, who lived in the desert, would come with our plans and we'd work through the night.

It was on an estate in Lafayette, where we had the privilege of staying six months, that I entertained all the folks who had befriended us. When we had to vacate that magnificent home, we stayed in a house in Berkeley, loaned to us while our friends were in Inverness. We then rented a charming little cottage in Orinda amidst a grove of pine trees. That was our home for the next nine months. It was only ten minutes from our property, where we spent most of our time. We were thrilled every time we drove through the Caldecott Tunnel to glimpse our Bay view. We knew, after having lived and traveled the world over, nothing could keep us from returning to our site.

I don't think I ever felt more a victim than during that first week after the fire when I went to Nordstrom's to buy underwear. A fire refugee ahead of me was sobbing and making such a scene that all the salesgirls were comforting her. As I stood in line, I was tempted to forego the ten percent discount the store was offering to fire victims, but my frugality won out and I admitted in a whisper that I, too, had lost my home.

The day after our fruitless search for a place to rent, we were accosted by the adjuster from the insurance company. He happened to be a little fellow flown out here from the Midwest. I guess our California home confounded him as he compared it to a little viewless shack on the back side of our hill and offered to settle for less than our home had been insured. We were mortally wounded that he would disparage our home; our home that we had built block by block; our wondrous home that had cradled us for 41 years; our home that foreign architects at the University extolled for retaining the soaring quality of a contemporary California home, while maintaining the strength and stability of European structures. We refused to deal with him and asked for another adjuster.

Henry immediately got in touch with Bob Stevens and asked him to bring up our original plans. Most people had no idea of what went into their lost homes, but with a complete set of plans and all the knowledge we had acquired building ours, Henry was certain we could come to an equitable agreement, and we were assured by our insurance agent that we could. Instead, we had to fight just to support the fact that we had a total loss, since our structure, because it was built of block, was still standing. That meant we had to pay an engineer to determine whether the fire had undermined our walls.

Through this worrisome time we were supported and comforted by our community. We were given clothing, and numerous fire meetings were arranged where we found solace in commiserating and exchanging ideas with our stressed out neighbors. We also had the backing of the United Policy Holders, a nonprofit organization whose main purpose is to help fire victims deal with their insurance companies. Even so, it took five different adjusters and countless meetings for us to finally settle our claim.

The next day, the personal property adjuster insisted upon meeting with me to make an inventory of our personal property losses. I started to chart the furniture arrangement in our living area, trying to recall every picture, vase and lamp. It took an hour for me to realize I was not up to the task. I begged to defer the agonizing exercise for a week.

After sitting around moping for a few days, I decided to take action by finding out the value of some of the things we had lost. My first trip was to Butterfield and Butterfield in San Francisco, where I took a photo my brother had sent me of the Persian prayer rug I had inherited from my grandfather. That was the rug our Armenian rug maker neighbor said he couldn't mend; that was the rug we then backed with canvas and later with plywood and hung on our fireplace wall, where its beauty of color was admired for years; that was the rug they said was worth thirty thousand dollars.

I went to the morgue of the Asian Museum in San Francisco with a photo of the brass oil lamp we had brought back from Ceylon. There I tracked down a picture in an ancient book that showed that our lamp was an exact replica of one made in the 5th century. Then I called the artist in Colombo, a prodigy who had grown up to become Sri Lanka's foremost painter, to find that our painting of his, "Spring Boks," was worth many times over what we had paid for it years ago.

My next trip was to the famous Gump's store in San Francisco with a small piece of a Havilland dinner plate that I found in the ruins. This is what remained of my favorite dishes growing up. Recently my mother had given me twelve of everything, including oyster dishes and consommé bowls with lids. I probably wouldn't have used them if I'd been told each dinner plate was worth one hundred and fifty dollars, so I'm glad I didn't know. The heirloom candlesticks we lost were twice as large as similar ones Gump's was exhibiting for $20,000. The loss of my thirty-five carat yellow sapphire ring, for which I paid thirty-five dollars at the Ratnapura mines in Ceylon, was the only piece of jewelry I mourned. There was no accounting for the many first editions I had received from my father's library, along with Ben Shawn's posters and a Heinemann print of mother and daughter. Suddenly, after the fact, we became aware for the first and last time of the material worth of what we had owned.

I don't want to appear ungrateful, as we really were very fortunate. Two months before the fire a good friend of mine who was in the insurance business, had suggested that for a few extra dollars we could get full replacement cost, instead of partial replacement, for our personal property. Our insurance company said our home was one year too old to qualify for that perk, so I changed to another insurance company, upgrading our policy and adding the replacement clause. In so doing, we might have been accused of setting the fire, since almost no one on the hill had thought to upgrade in years.

We had no intention of replacing our newly revalued lost treasures, but then we were told if we didn't replace in like kind, we were out of luck. The insurance company would pay only for the items we replaced. That was when Diane Feinstein rushed a bill through Congress, which permitted people who had a total loss to use their personal property stipend in any way they wished. That freed us to put much of our personal property money into replacing thirty-two mature oaks and landscaping our property. We then could use what was left for simple minimal replacement of the material things we had lost.

We were surprised and delighted to find some treasures among the ruins: the copper tray from Ceylon that was double glazed by the fire, giving it an unusual and interesting patina finish; the ceramic temple dogs brought to us at Brent School in the Philippines by our ambassador from Vietnam (ironically, meant to protect our household, but which instead elected to save themselves). It was only later, when I looked at the bank in front of our ravaged house, that I noticed little bits of scorched paper. Even after the conflagration and the rains, these scraps preserved the best short story I had ever written. This seemed such a miracle to me, I thought of sending it to the <u>Atlantic Monthly</u>, noting that this story doesn't want to die, so publish it. Best of all, our son had driven out over the flames as he tried to rescue neighbors and he was safe, although we lost our kitty. Our few surviving treasures reminded us that possessions are expendable and to take joy in what we had.

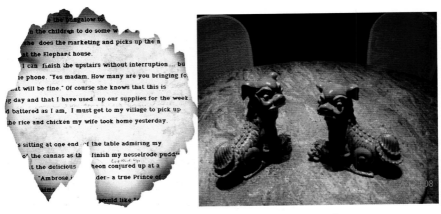

A story fragment, and the temple dogs – survivors of the fire.

VIEW

Beginning All Over Again

There we were, on our lot, Henry, Bob and I, the original triumvirate, forty-four years after we had laid the string line for our original home, eager and excited about staking out our home once again. It was a reverent and awesome moment.

Although Bob's original plans were extremely helpful in settling with the insurance company, it still took many frustrating meetings to come to an equitable agreement; and that brought us to December, a terrible month to begin building, with the wind, the rain and the penetrating cold. But we didn't have the courage to start until we knew what we had to work with.

This was a tough period for us: having our golf clubs stolen from the trunk of our car, the only possession, other than the car, that we had left; battling numerous claims adjusters; living in six different rentals, remembering the things we could never replace while working with Bob to redesign a home for our present needs. Forty-four years older and hopefully wiser, if not as agile for toting block, we were ready. Throwing caution to the winds, I said, "Bob, create a new home for us. The sky's the limit."

This time he was into planning a luxuriant inside garden bordering a glassed-in dining area, revolving around a huge kitchen that would be the core of the house. We were in awe of his magnificent conception, until I realized I couldn't function in a home where I would be the major attraction while preparing dinner, and that an indoor garden made no sense in temperate Berkeley, where we live outdoors year round.

Henry was captivated by the exotic plan, as were all who saw it. So I had to be the one to reject Bob's wondrous fantasy. But how could I do so without injuring his grand vision and artistic soul? Finally I said, "Bob, no matter how exciting your new blueprint is, there is nothing that can touch your original house plan. We must have it back." I know he was disappointed, but he was flattered, too.

So we kept to the original footprint, only incorporating small changes that we learned over the years would make our living more comfortable. We flipped the living and dining areas, and instead of having the great cantilevered fireplace, which smoked the house when the wind blew the wrong way, we had a more conventional dividing fireplace wall. We also decided to have our bedroom on the east side of the house, which was private and sunny in the morning, even though we had to forsake the new moon sitting over the Bay. The beauty of staying with our original design was that, even with its many modern upgrades, when it was finished, we knew we had come back to our very own home.

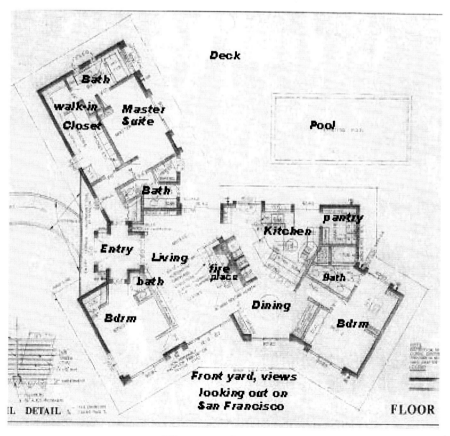

The new house plan

We adored our original block house because it was so solid and silent and organic. It was difficult to forego the strength and soundproofing it had afforded us over the decades. But now we knew the home we had built to endure for eternity had not endured. We also had to admit, though reluctantly, using block instead of wood left a lot to be desired in terms of insulation. So we decided to tell Bob to proceed with designing a conventional frame house.

Every evening as we walked the hills and saw houses being built of green wood, we spent sleepless nights imagining the shrinking and creaking of those wet timbers and, in a few years, the invasion of termites. Then one night we went to a neighborhood fire meeting and previewed a film featuring a material that had been developed in Austria in 1968 and was just now being introduced to America.

The material looked like block, but was made of cement buds mixed with Styrofoam. It was structurally strong, virtually fireproof, and highly insulated. We were so excited about the attributes of this new material, Rastra, that we drove down to Riverside, California, to visit the factory the next day.

When we arrived at the factory, we were given the underwriter's lab report, which explained how Rastra was erected, then reinforced and poured with cement in the vertical and horizontal cores, and allowed to cure for seven days. We saw how the wall was put in a press with 200 pounds per square feet and a flame applied to its face for a period of two hours. At the end of that time, the temperature rise on the other side of the wall was a quarter of a degree Fahrenheit; the horizontal deflection at the center of the wall was just a quarter of an inch, proving its strength and resistance to fire. The International Conference of Building Officials approved Rastra for homes and apartments. Certainly, we could do no less.

We also observed the automatic process for forming Rastra units. The material was extruded into 10 foot lengths, 15 inches high and 10 inches wide, with a 6 inch core for reinforced steel on 15 inch centers, both horizontally and vertically. Each unit was light enough for two men to carry and put in place.

Then we were given a tour of a 6,000 square foot Southwestern style mansion, built entirely of Rastra. We observed how the forms had been erected, glued and braced until they were poured, and how the material could be grooved to accept electrical wiring and pipes. The raw surface was then finished with plaster. We learned how easy it was to make arches, to add-on for headboards, bookshelves and other architectural details.

We called Bob from the factory to tell him to stop work on his drawings for our wood frame house, that we would pay him for his time to redo the plans. We told him we were determined to use this new material and would send him the specifications. We suggested he make a trip to the factory to learn all he could about Rastra.

We didn't even wait for approval from the city of Oakland. Cavalier, indeed! We should have been concerned that the city fathers wouldn't give us permission to use Rastra. In ordinary times we had been told it could take years to approve a new material. Fortunately, the city engineers, after familiarizing themselves with the report from the ICBM, were eager to have us introduce Rastra to the fire zone.

Now we could have a house with all the qualities of our original block home, with many more refinements. Before, the block was rough and exposed, and we'd painted and struck the joints to achieve texture and warmth. Our Rastra home would be plastered, achieving a similar, but more elegant effect.

Rastra construction: quick to erect, strong, insulating, flexible, and fire-resistant.

On the job, morning till night

Using polystyrene foam blocks to build your home

Photo by Chris Duffey

Elaine and Henry McGee's home is one of only four in Northern California to be built using Rastra brand polystyrene building blocks.

BY TERESA FERGUSON SCOTT

Rebuilding in the East Bay Hills presents an extraordinary opportunity to try a variety of new construction products. Some projects that took more time to design are using new building materials for improved fire-resistance, energy efficiency and better seismic strengthening.

One such material is polystyrene — the same plastic foam your coffee comes in. But Rastra, the manufacturer of the product, claims to employ 100-percent recycled plastic foam, most of which came from McDonalds before its corporate decision to use coated paper cups instead.

The construction industry is basically

This material is being used by Rastra for the foundations and walls at the McGee residence and guesthouse at 1350 Grandview Drive. Although this type of foam product has been used extensively in Europe for years, Rastra representatives say the McGee residence is only one of four installations in Northern California homes.

According to Rastra, a strong timber lobby plus building officials' lack of familiarity with the product has limited its use in the United States. The City of Oakland's Building Department, however, has been supportive and encourages use of the product. This may be due in part to polystyrene's fire-resistant qualities.

Preparing the foundation

Rastra piers

121

Do We or Don't We

When we suffered a mudslide in 1964, we contemplated using a contractor to replace the deck that had tumbled into the canyon. Although we were covered by slide insurance in those days, we couldn't face the thought of contracting the job when we knew we could do it for half the price. In 1992, after losing our home, we were faced with the same choice. Henry said reluctantly, "If we were ten years younger, we'd do it ourselves. I think we had better let a contractor do it this time." We lived to regret that decision.

On the recommendation of a neighbor, we interviewed a personable young contractor who seemed interested and enthusiastic about working with our new material. We felt it imperative that he go to the factory to learn all he could about Rastra. He promised he would take advantage of our offer to send him to Riverside before starting the job. On that basis we hired him and planned his trip. However, he reneged. The best we could do was to arrange for a representative from the Rastra factory to come up to give him some instruction.

Our young contractor thought he knew it all, which proved to be a problem throughout the building process. Henry and I spent our days from early morning till sundown on the job, checking his and his inexperienced workers' every move. We used our weekends to redo or tidy up the loose ends the workers left undone. And finally, we took back a number of the subcontracting jobs ourselves:

the tile, the marble, the plastering, the ceiling, the heating system, the roof. We would have felt much less stress and would have been so much more satisfied, had we done the whole job ourselves.

We didn't even save our old bones by using a general contractor. One day I heard Henry come into our rental in Orinda. When I asked why he was home so early, he mumbled something and went into the bathroom. I later learned that he had gone down to the filter house, which was on the steep slope of our hill, lost his footing and tumbled fifty feet to the bottom of the canyon, bumping through and over all kinds of debris left by the fire. None of the workman knew that he had fallen, so he had to climb up all those fifty feet on his own. Luckily, he hadn't broken any bones. But, for an eighty year-old chap, that was quite a feat, especially to come out of such a terrible fall with only a few scratches.

Walls braced for pouring

The one plus in rebuilding was that both we and the city of Oakland were much more attuned to the need for energy conservation in 1992 than we were in 1948. Bob designed our homes so that we received lots of natural sun, and we now incorporated double-paned glass, highly insulated walls and roof, and solar panels for heating the pool.

The only beef I had with our original home was the radiant heat. For my internal thermostat, it never accommodated well enough to the swings in temperature in the Bay Area. This time we could install an ordinary forced-air heating system and I'd be warm, at last.

Then Bob came up with a new idea for heating called Air Floor, though I'm told it was used by Koreans centuries ago. Hot air is circulated through channels under the slab, warming the cement, and the warm air also comes up through vents in the floor. This combination, of radiant heating through the floors and blown air in the rooms from a central furnace, seemed to be an answer to my prayers. Still, I was skeptical that heat would be delivered as quickly as a forced-air system. After visiting St. Mary's Church in Moraga, which had installed the Air Floor system, I learned that the heat was fine where people kneeled, but the extremities of the large building were not adequately warmed. Henry was adamant about having warm floors, so he fell for the system. I was equally unyielding about warm rooms, so I was determined to resist.

This time my partners passionately opposed me. I had to capitulate, but not without a knock down, drag out fight. Happily, our Air Floor System has been a success. It's efficient, delivers the heat adequately and is extremely quiet.

Installing the air floor

Furnishing Again

We delighted in the architectural features of Bob's design, which had to do double duty, to make up for all the memorabilia we had collected and lost over a lifetime. That's why the choice of materials, colors and textures became an even more important and integral part of our home this time.

Of course, for me, scrambling for materials was the fun of building. Bob and I learned that our favorite lumber company had just received a load of Philippine mahogany. That was just what we wanted for our ceiling. By hand, we picked each two by six board foot, enough to cover our entire ceiling. In San Francisco, I found a delicate peach marble for my bathroom. I also fell in love with an Italian tile for our floor, but there wasn't enough in stock. The owner tried to tempt me into using another tile, which was almost but not quite right. It was much less expensive and was on hand; this time, though, I wasn't lured by a bargain, and he promised to order what I needed from Italy. I found another exquisite marble for our fireplace, which we also used on the long counter in the dining area. Bob came up with a handsome handmade blue-green tile that we used on some surfaces in the kitchen, on the fireplace ledge, around the pool, and on the outside table and counter.

With our guaranteed replacement clause in our insurance policy, we had the right to replace our personal property at today's cost. But even with all that backing, I soon made a horrendous mistake. After taking a year to research appliances, I finally made my selection at Wicks in Berkeley, a well-established institution. When it came time to have the appliances delivered, I paid with my Visa card. No sooner had I gotten home than Wicks called to say they would prefer a check and they would credit my Visa. Shortly after that, I heard rumors that Wicks was in financial trouble. Then I received my bank statement, showing that Wicks had not canceled my payment. And then we heard that Wicks was declaring bankruptcy.

With our family cars and my daughter's landscaping truck, we raced down to the warehouse. My daughter was dumbfounded to see her tentative, laid back mother run through the storage facility pointing to this refrigerator and that dishwasher, saying we'll take this and that as Henry and our sons put the selections on dollies and wheeled them to our vehicles. Immediately after we loaded the equipment, the warehouse doors closed. The moral of that story is to get a receipt when canceling a payment before writing another check. However, from then on, furnishing our home, while an awesome challenge, was a joyous one. I might add, in time, we recouped our Visa charge.

As I wander about our home, on a dark and gloomy day so many years later, I am buoyed by the warmth within. And then I stop to marvel at what color can achieve. All the while we were rebuilding, Bob kept talking about the "banana color" he saw for our walls. Somehow, the color of the peel of the banana didn't appeal to me. Luckily,

I held my tongue. What he was talking about was the rich creamy color of the banana itself. That is the color we used throughout the living areas.

When I visit rebuilt homes on the hill, the stark white walls of most of them are uninviting and cold. What a difference our color makes! Our place just glows with its banana walls and subtle variations. In the entrance there is a deeper shade, entering the den there is a dusty hue, my bedroom is peachier, and the guest room is rosy. Everyone feels the depth and the quality of light as they roam about without being conscious of the exquisite shadings that perform this miracle.

As you take a tour with me, you enter into the great hall, a space Bob designed at the insistence of our kids, so that people wouldn't enter through the dining room's sliding doors. This area added 300 square feet to the original footage, and many more dollars to our tax bill, and still everyone enters through the dining room doors in the front. There, on the floor, is a rug from Nepal. It should feel privileged to be there, as I tried a dozen other carpets before I chose this one. Above a simple wrought iron, travertine-topped table in the hall, is a copy of Rousseau's "A Carnival Night." The original painting belonged to my father's best friend who gave us the first print, which was made in Switzerland, as our wedding present. Luckily, the Philadelphia Museum had copies, so there it hangs today, nicely mounted, but not up to our original Gump's frame.

To the left as you enter the living area is a little Clavinova. It's not the quality of the Yamaha piano we sacrificed a summer vacation to buy so many years ago, and it isn't the baby grand Bob wanted us to have, but it fits and its electronic keyboard is fun to play.

On the living room floor is the Chinese rug that almost ruptured our fifty-year marriage. By chance, I came upon this rug that melded all our colors, was the right dimension - and was 50% percent reduced. Henry felt betrayed because he said I had broken our pact to purchase nothing until we had a house in which to put things. But I dragged him to the store, where he immediately wrote a check. What's more, we bought another rug for the study.

As I have written earlier, I recreated my own family's great oversized couch for our original home, which turned out to be too deep for comfortable seating. This time I intended to do better. Why then, did I fall in love with a leather sofa in an Italian catalog? But I did, ordering two, with the stipulation that, should these not accommodate us, the owner would put them in his showroom. They worked, though, even in the dusty pink leather they came in by mistake.

Bob had a six-foot round glass-top table, which he willingly donated for the cost of sending it up from Palm Springs. Henry felt the size was a bit much for a coffee table, and he was right; but I loved it, so he went along. It now does double-duty as the overflow Thanksgiving table for all those spry enough to sit on the floor.

The Seniors Writing Group around the six foot glass coffee table

Set for Thanksgiving

I was fortunate to find a large granite slab for the dining table that incorporated all of our colors. I had it cut to a six-foot round along with a three foot round for the turntable. All we had to do was get five strong able bodies to lift the heavy granite onto a drainage pipe.

The real trouble was finding dining chairs to enhance that unique table. I couldn't imagine what they should look like until I saw a lone chair in the corner of Breuners during its annual sellout sale. The graceful rattan backed chair was marked $69 from $527. When I asked if there were others, I was told to look around. I found four more, marked $269. The sales person said she would have to give them to me for the lowest price. Bob purchased five more from the factory for the wholesale price. They are just right and can be used about the house as well.

The dining table and chairs

Henry and I went to the old San Francisco company, McCroskey, for our beds. We chose extra long twins that we pushed together, which can be raised or lowered. These came with a twenty-year warranty. We became mechanical engineers when we climbed into bed with all the gadgets, one to handle the bed, another to click on the fire, and a third to manage the TV. But it is worth the trouble.

Walking through a showroom one day, I flopped on a sumptuous queen size bed, which I had to have for our guest room. Imagine my surprise when I learned that it was a waterbed. I bought it anyway, and to this day, our guests are more amazed than I was when I tell them they are sleeping on water.

This time it took a great deal of research to find the right covering for our sliding glass doors. We finally settled on vertical blinds, which sounds terribly mundane but proves Bob's point; that with imagination, any material with the right color, texture and proper application can be spectacular. Of course, nothing can take the place of our original draperies.

Looking through the kitchen to the pool area

Mounted on either side of the double doors at the front entry are two temple lion dogs Bob brought back from Burma. They're supposed to welcome visitors, but instead, do a good job of frightening little children.

All our other decorative energy went into filling our bookshelves. It was great fun to feel that with each book we picked, we were replenishing our library and enhancing the beauty of our home. As for everything else, we are still filling in. It isn't until we need a safety pin that we go out and buy a bunch.

When we moved into our home in December 1994, Bob left. Here is his letter from Southern California. I think it is a testament us all.

Dear Henry and Elaine,

I'm sending my love and sincere appreciation for your being such a part of my life! The trust you had in me to recreate a home for you has given me some new powers. Ideas seem to flow fluently. I guess there is no end to the growth of our complicated minds.

I wish to thank you both for the many things you have done for me in those last few years in being together again -. Surely your lives are daily strengthened by such consideration towards mankind.

I thank you for the job -- I thank you for the money -- I thank God for being part of the six McGees.

May the New Year be paved with fun, happiness, and great health! May those loving floors and walls be my arms -- for I will always hold you dear. With much love, Your Architect,

ROBERT WEAVER STEVENS   *Bob*

134

Roofing Problems

All through this memoir I have been glorifying our do-it-yourself house building. Perhaps to encourage other owner builders, I have glossed over some of the pitfalls and heartaches we encountered along the way. The fact is, a number of friends have built because of our example. But all the blood sweat and tears, all the learning by doing, all the building skills acquired over four decades were for naught, when we were faced with the flooding of our new home, three years after rebuilding.

The very last words Henry spoke to me were, "Get Flagler up on our roof!" That was in December of '97, the week before he died. And that command wasn't easy to accomplish. I finally threatened our contractor that his reputation would be ruined when rain would pour in on all of Berkeley attending Henry's memorial. Only then did he do a major repair job on what I considered a brand new roof.

Our sad saga began when Bob fashioned an unorthodox roof with great overhangs, a tower, sweeping views and lots of skylights. We fell in love with the beautiful lichen green of the cement tile, but their fragility, combined with the low pitched roof and the botched workmanship of the roofers, permitted rain to flood our guest bathroom and kitchen. Fortunately, the ceiling allowed the rain to flow through the grooves, and Bob was able to treat the mahogany with a wash that prevented serious staining. Our Italian tile floors accepted the rain easily and our Chinese rugs escaped with little damage.

Jose, who ran the roofing job, was an obliging fellow, and he assured us that whenever we had leaks he would fix them and no one would have to know. Unfortunately, they occurred regularly, right from the start. And that was our first mistake - to be in cahoots with the foreman and not the contractor.

In 2000, three years after Henry died, tiles began flying off the roof. Flagler told me that the tiles were insured to 60 miles an hour, and insisted our winds were gusting to 80 mph so they were not responsible. I was able to convince him otherwise after speaking to Bay Area meteorologist Mike Pechner, who said that only on the top of Grizzly Peak were 80 mile winds recorded, in 1989; 700 feet below, protected by hills and our oaks, we might have winds that gust to 50 miles per hour at most. Foolishly, I agreed to pay $3500 for a supply of replacement tiles, after I was assured that such payment would not negate our ten-year warranty.

Two years later tiles were flying off the roof again, and I was alarmed that they might cause injury. It was at that point that a well-known roofer in our neighborhood advised me to engage an independent roof consultant. With the costly analysis of the Webster Associates report in hand, I understood why our roof had caused us so much distress. The consultant listed six major installation errors that needed to be corrected to bring our roof up to code, essentially requiring a new roof.

We contacted Flagler's insurance companies, who sent out their adjusters. They wriggled out of their responsibilities, claiming we hadn't reported the leakage within three years of installation, even though we now had proof that the installation was not up to code from the beginning.

Catching the leaks

All during this stressful time, I was looking into roofing companies and getting bids. At a builders' convention, I spoke to the president of our original roofing company, who offered to replace our tiles free of charge. That was tempting, but now I was convinced cement tile was not appropriate for our roof.

I saw a magnificent copper roof in Montclair done in what is called the Bermuda style. That roof convinced me that a metal roof was the answer. It's ironic that had we done the roof in expensive copper at the outset we would have been ahead in cost and trouble. Our kids have lost part of their inheritance, but Henry would approve of our new roof and Bob would swoon over the muted color.

Initial concrete tile roof

Metal replacement roof

Alas, Henry isn't around to chide me for my omissions, to challenge my elaborations and exaggerations or to check the technical aspects of our building project. I was counting on a collaborative effort in the editing of this memoir because that's how we lived our life together. But I'm eternally grateful that we were able to spend his last three years together in our paradise on our hill.

Ode to Henry

I love your robust and enduring presence
Your striving for perfection in all things
Your intensity, etching each moment
Your impulsive and often courageous way
Of acting, no matter the consequence.
I love your capacity to live in the here and now
Your single-minded loyalty and commitment
Your keen kinesthetic sense
Your heroic ability to surmount whatever
you are dealt, without whining.
The pride and optimism that carried you
To the very end and beyond, so majestically.
I even miss your short fuse,
your need for approval,
Your dislike of negatives
But most of all,
I love your deep caring and your passion.
Gone is the spice in my life.

Our daughter Diane gave this beautiful tribute to Henry at his memorial: "...Dad was a doer, not a talker, except when he was wearing his instructor's hat. The depth of his feelings was articulated by action, rather than by words, evidenced in such things as the houses he constructed and the adventures he engaged us in. Dad's legacy is that of experience, of accepting challenges and overcoming obstacles, of taking risks and pioneering, of doing the undoable and of fixing the unfixable. In these ways he was not only the most successful man I know, he was heroic. He was a lesson in resourcefulness, determination, resilience, creativity, courage and devotion, and his life described the rewards of following the dictates of one's conscience and one's heart."

Flowers for Henry's memorial on our table

Maintaining Our Home and Honoring Bob

Passing the Elmwood Hardware store this morning, I happened to see in their window a bamboo rake for leaves. Nostalgia set in as it reminded me of a similar bamboo rake Bob insisted I buy to nurture the Firth wool turf rug in our original home. I well remember, during a home tour, a couple exclaiming about our beautiful wall-to-wall carpets. My husband fervently and with great pride shocked them, and embarrassed me, by saying, "These rugs so maintain themselves that my wife almost never needs to vacuum." I must admit, before guests arrived, I would whip through the house with that rake, when I should have been vacuuming. But the rake so stimulated the fibers and so enlivened and perked up the shag, that I relegated the vacuum to the back of the broom closet much of the time. What's more, that original rug lasted many years more than it should have, due, I'm convinced, to the massaging I gave it.

As for our interconnected dining and kitchen areas, Bob insisted that I have a sink full of soapy water in which to dump the dishes, so they would be out of sight as they were taken from the dining table. Of course, hanging our Revere Ware pots on the fireplace wall was very convenient, even if it meant we had to shine the bottoms after each use. We didn't mind the extra elbow grease, as the copper of the pots was an integral part of our color scheme, adding a decorative and aesthetic touch to the overall decor.

Which reminds me, as I have said over and over again, our philosophy was to live simply, in an aesthetically pleasing environment with the least amount of effort. The last part of that sentence was where we got into hot water. Bob bought us a squeegee, which he implored us to use after each shower. We thought it was a needless expenditure of energy. Besides, it didn't add anything to the beauty of our home, like shining the pots did. And so we showered to our hearts' content year after year. At long last, when we could no longer abide the gummy, spattered, opaque glass shower doors, we tried scrubbing them with every chemical available. They were doomed to remain a disgrace. We learned our lesson, though; in our rebuilt home, we have not one squeegee but two in the bathrooms, and we consider them a gift for keeping our shower glass doors clear. The squeegee also has a way of keeping us in shape by bending and stretching after each shower. We even try to convince our guests to exercise along with us!

If it weren't for Bob's tutelage, I never would have had the courage to see possibilities in ordinary materials. Spotting a box of twelve by twelve combed wooden squares in a dusty corner of Piedmont Lumber, I determined they would make an interesting bedroom ceiling for our first house. Bob not only endorsed the find, but embellished the material by setting them in a checkerboard pattern, which made them literally come alive. I remember the joy I felt, while nursing my youngest, as I

142

watched the reflected light from the pool dance on those checkerboard squares.

Perhaps the find that pleases me most is the Italian marble I uncovered while rebuilding. With only two boxes, the shop owner thought he didn't have enough for any kind of a job. He literally gave the marble to me. Bob, of course, was able to figure, to the last piece, how he could decorate two of our bathrooms.

Marble tile in the baths   **Dining chair**

After designing our dining room table, I came across suitable chairs. The seats were covered with a beautiful green silk material shot through with copper. When Bob said those sheer delicate seat covers would never do for our casual style of living, I was hurt to the quick. Of course we would be careful of those fragile seat covers. But Bob insisted that we have them recovered with durable, washable Naugahyde in a delicious coral color. How right he was! To this day they look like new, while the delicate silk, taken off the chairs, languishes and grows old in my bottom dresser drawer.

But more important than the details of selecting and maintaining materials were the overall concepts we gained from working with Bob. We learned, for example, to choose materials that we liked and go with them throughout the house. That's why our hardware, the hinges, the door knobs, the bathroom faucets, the tracks for our draperies, are all brushed aluminum. The same goes for color. Although we have subtle distinctions throughout, all blend into each other. Flow and harmony dominated his every choice. That sense of unity and balance is hard to define but is truly there. Everyone who experiences our home seems to feel it, and I especially, who am totally unfit to live anywhere else.

The extra long twin beds we'd pushed together were a stark reminder of my crushing loss, as I fought the clutter of pillows bunched up on Henry's side and lay crumpled and alone on my own. For two years I found the bedroom unbearable; I couldn't wait for Bob's promised visit to come up with an original and affordable solution. Then Bob died, on January 1, 2000.

And so we gathered to celebrate Bob's life, protected from the searing Palm Springs sun under his grapefruit tree. We were an odd assortment. All of his adult nieces and nephews were there to honor their beloved uncle who brought color, spice and romance into their lives. There were families like ours, whose lives were changed forever after working with Bob. Artists and professors from the unique community of Pinyon Crest, 2,000 feet above the valley, came to pay their respects. All of us bereft and wondering how we would cope without this original, talented and generous, though terribly flawed when it came to money, genius of a man.

Everyone had a story to tell. His nephews and nieces related the story of how Bob came to Thanksgiving dinner and had them help him cut the legs off the dining room table. He then sawed the beautiful mahogany tabletop in half to make a headboard and side table for their parents' bedroom. When their mother came from the kitchen with the turkey, there was no table on which to place the bird. The story is more horrendous for those of us who knew his very proper and fastidious sister.

Dorry Phillips, a neighbor, told how Bob found a part of a bumper on the road outside her house in Pinyon Crest, brought it in and proceeded to twist and polish it. And there it sits where he placed it, a unique decorative piece on her mantle.

Vicki McDermott, a colleague, begged Bob to teach her how to make popovers. He not only made her famous for popovers, he showed her how to make them in his collection of iron receptacles once used by cobblers for nails.

The neighbor who boards horses, which plagued Bob with smells and flies, has planted a swath of fruit trees along her border in memory of her beloved friend.

A Bit of History

In the early Twenties, a developer with imagination decided to put roads and utilities in the upper Claremont Heights area and sell lots as summer retreats for San Franciscans. The project had hardly gotten off the ground when the Crash came. It has been incomprehensible to me that one of the most beautiful areas in the East Bay had not been developed since 1929. But, of course, hard times forestalled further development, until we bought our lot and began to build in 1948.

When the 1991 Firestorm swept across our hill, it wasn't the first time in this century that our area had been ravaged. A major fire decimated the Berkeley Hills in 1923, and smaller fires occurred in 1946 and 1970.

The week we moved into our home in 1950, I watched, fascinated but frozen, as a bulldozer tore into the bank across from us. It took the city two days, after I called them, to stop the owner from reconstituting the hill to his own specifications. This one wildcat operation has caused landslides, slippage and drainage problems in our neighborhood for over fifty years. After a prolonged rainy season in the fifties, Henry and I, walking on Grand View Drive, were inches away from being buried under a mudslide directly related to that excavation.

Since we were the only residents on our side of the hill for years, I was extremely spoiled and protective of our privacy. If even one stray car happened down our steep little road, I would get goose pimples. For that reason I didn't mind that we had almost no home delivery and would have to hike down to the bottom of the hill to pick up mail and the newspaper. I was especially beholden to our crippled milkman, who was loyal and courageous enough to give us delivery every other day for our four babies. Gradually, a few pioneer types bought in our territory. By 1967, we had formed a Grand View Drive Association of thirteen homeowners, which gave us some clout with the city when we wanted to fix potholes in the road or address street lighting and parking.

I still remember the thrill I felt when breaking ground on our lot. Just the smell of moist loam, as it was turned over on the bulldozer's blade, sent me into raptures. Early on, as each new lot was readied for building, I would run up to the site and get that same skidding sensation. Even breathing in dank, moist earth in a little village in Ceylon made me feel wonderfully at home and at peace.

In the fifties we saw earth-moving equipment at work on the adjoining hill. We realized that Mr. Hiller's plans for a gated community were intended to prevent egress from our hill through his exclusive development. My neighbor and I donned our best duds and went to the Planning Commission in Oakland. After hearing our plea for another way out of the hills in case of fire, all but one member voted to stop the Hiller project until a connection was included in his plans. Mr. Hiller's friend on the committee was outraged: "How can you let two young women charm you into a quick decision without hearing Mr. Hiller's side of the story?" Nevertheless, the vote stood.

In June of 1997, five decades later, I came before the city council again. I asked that they rescind a recent order that gave total authority to the Design Review Department with no right of appeal by residents, except through the courts. I reminded them of how many more lives might have been lost in the 1991 fire if we hadn't had the right to appear before the council in the fifties. I told them that the majority of fire survivors had rebuilt, but speculators now coming into the area had little sensitivity for the environment; that residents and builders must have the opportunity to meet to iron out such problems as drainage, views, off-street parking and the like.

Today, so many years after I appeared before the Planning Commission and the morning after throwing a Fourth of July party for our neighbors, I offer everyone a silent apology for ranting and raving. After all, recent homeowners didn't have the pick of the hill, they had to buy homes on steep slopes with little access to outdoor living. I don't get goose pimples anymore when six families drive up and down our little road, I don't even notice them. It has taken me a half-century to accept my husband's philosophy that everyone should have the joy that we have had of living in paradise.

Metamorphosis of our Site: 1948-2008

Surveying the oak tree that survived the fire of 1991 and remembering the soil we had carelessly pushed against its trunk in 1948, my mind whirls back to all the changes we have wrought on our own property over a half-century.

In 1950, we constructed a spectacular walkway of railroad ties wending from the top of Grand View Drive through the oaks to our front door. We willingly gave up outdoor living rather than cut the trees that hugged the protected side of our home. It took us two years to sacrifice a few of those great oaks in order to gain a vast, level, outdoor living area. During those years, we planted our canyon with a hundred little pines and a number of golden rain trees, courtesy of the State Agricultural Department. The pines didn't survive, but we still have a few golden rain trees, and more recently, we have planted a grove of redwoods, in honor of Henry.

Today I am sitting in our patio area, next to a lap pool and spa with lots of space for swimming, dining and entertaining. It's odd that I have neglected to write about the building of the pool, as it was a more difficult project than building our home Since it was on the edge of a fifty-foot drop into our canyon, the great challenge was to brace the east wall of the pool for pouring concrete forms and to carve out a filter house below. However, with

Henry's ingenuity and his newly acquired building skills, he was able to surmount all obstacles.

The original pool, patio, spa and guesthouse

The rebuilt pool and patio

I still hear children's voices echoing across the canyon, "Marco Polo," "Marco Polo." That pool was my nemesis as well as my savior. It was my nemesis, because with four children under four, alone on our mountain, and even with a fence surrounding the pool, I was always counting heads. Almost until they were grown, I would suddenly scream, "Where is Phillip?" startling my poor husband out of his wits. But it was also my savior, as it made of our home a vacation resort. Of course, it also made misfits of our kids when we went for a week to the Lair of the Bear. Suddenly, I found myself trying to catch all four as they scampered around the University of California pool in the nude. Today our nude swimming is confined to after hours in our built up neighborhood.

And now I glance at the far end of the pool where I see Japanese maples gracing the backdrop. If I squint, I conjure up a little guest cottage housing my oldest son and a sauna room with the heater we brought back from Sweden in 1965. Since the fire, that guesthouse has been moved to the lower level.

Glancing through the glass doors in the front study, I view a putting green bordered by a rosemary hedge. We included it so that if ever Henry couldn't get to the golf course, he would be able to putt at home. It seems but yesterday that we had a lawn in that area, with an exposed aggregate concrete path running around the border for wagons and bikes.

As I move under the shade of the tree outside our bedroom, I muse about the gnarled oak that graced that spot in olden days. When it decided to die, we replaced it with a flowering pear and when that tree gave up, we planted a Red Delicious apple tree. Today we have a Robinia tree growing so tall we may have to replace it when it shades the solar panels on the roof.

Miraculously, one old oak which bordered our canyon and sheltered us from the road, survived the fire. That oak was covered with brown leaves when we returned from Ceylon in 1968. The arborist warned us that the soil we had allowed to settle around its trunk was choking it to death. Twenty-five years after he first worked for us, we called Mr. Steltor to the rescue. He not only scraped the soil away from the trunk, he built a basin of stone around its base. Today it is a magnificent specimen that not only gives us pleasure and privacy, but is the main feature for the house across the canyon.

The pool area today, landscaped by daughter Suzanne

While clearing our lot of coyote brush, preparatory to building our first home, Henry came across what he thought might be an oak. From that little seedling grew a giant oak in just the right spot to frame and protect us from the western sun. When I came up after the fire to view our ruins with the insurance adjuster, she accused me of ignoring all our other losses as I walked up to that tree and shouted gleefully, "I think it will live!" The following ditty tells its tragic tale.

Clearing our land my husband spoke
"I think I've nicked a little oak"
"Save it!" I shouted
The bulldozer man pouted,
"Avoiding that weed will cost a pretty penny."
"No matter," we replied, "its only money."
Four decades pass
Towering over our home
A majestic Oak has grown
Its shimmering leaves sheltered and screened
Our home, from the western sun, redeemed.
In a blaze of 2000 degrees
Its trunk scorched beyond reprieve
Our Oak must be replaced
Else our property remains defaced.
With arborist, laborers and crane
A worthy replacement was obtained.
A year passed
Our little oak grew straight and true
Perhaps we'd live to see it tower anew.
Over night brown leaves appeared
Then more and we feared
"The roots need water," warned the arborist
"The roots are too wet," opined the agronomist
Confused and powerless we watch with dismay
As seared leaves increase day by day.
But, dare we hope when way up high
We see a wisp of green against the sky
We pray for heavenly intervention
After all,
"Poems are made by fools like me
*But only God can make a tree." ***

*Last 2 lines from the poem, 'The Trees' by Joyce Kilmer.

158

*Our mighty oak before and after the fire,
and its replacement.*

Our lower level has undergone many transformations as well. In the beginning, we planted a fruit orchard; unfortunately, the birds harvested the fruit before we could. We were more successful with artichokes, but our best venture was raising chickens. Early on, we built a carport area with room to park fifteen cars for faculty parties. Today, we again have a large parking area and have planted thirteen young oaks bordering the property. Our guest cottage is snuggled in the back. Despite the warning from the arborist that the two oaks sheltering the cottage would certainly die in a few years and our insurance wouldn't cover their loss, I was prepared to strap myself to those trees to prevent their demise. Contrary to the prediction of the specialist, they are growing and prospering

The guesthouse with its oak trees

One of the features of our original home was the forest of oaks on that lower level. It was sheer delight for us, and our guests, to amble through the grove up to our house. The fire consumed them all.

The Redwood tie path through the oaks,
before and after the fire.

The rebuilt entry stairs.

An aerial picture was taken of our property in 1994. It shows a barren landscape, and well it should, as we had lost thirty-two oak trees, some maples, a magnificent madrone tree and so much more. It's my contention that oaks are survivors. Today, an old oak in the canyon whose trunk was hollowed out by an ancient fire appears to be enjoying a robust life. Perhaps it's our oak trees that have given us the strength and spirit to survive the loss of our home and all the material things we cherished.

Aerial view of our rebuilt home and guest cottage -1994

It has been over fourteen years since we moved back. Along with the three oaks that survived, we are making a comeback, thanks to my landscaper daughter, who has made our property flower again. It has taken me a lifetime to realize that everything evolves and blossoms over time and not to mourn too long, but rather, go with the flow.

EPILOG

To My Very Own Henry

No firestorm can wrench you from our soil

Nor diminish your hard work and toil

That built our wondrous home

From which we'll never roam.

There's no ending, all is still pending

For In my heart, this is just a start.

As long as I'm alive, you'll help me strive

And when I'm no more, we'll both explore

The cosmos together and relish the next endeavor.